TO BRENTON & EMBERLY

Always remember to look both ways in life, but <u>smile</u> when you finally get to where you're going.

INTRODUCTION: GRANDMA'S OLD TYPEWRITER

I love to type; I always have.

Maybe it's the idea of creating something from a blank sheet of paper, or just being able to release your thoughts. But something about shooting lyrical lightning from furious fingertips is really refreshing. And when you get into a rhythm? It's like a bunch of little fireworks going off, one after the other.

It's that passion that led me to pursue writing as a career. So, as a kid, a typewriter wasn't just a really cool invention, it was a key to the future. And as primitive as they may seem now, that singular, basic device is responsible for billions of published words over the course of human history.

So, I guess you could say I'm a huge supporter of the serial printer. A 'Stan' for the steno-graph.

Having said that, when it comes to typing these days? Things seem to have shifted. The keys just don't feel the same way that they used to. For some reason, they don't have the same smooth texture, or the exact popping sound that I distinctly remember as a kid. And where did that bell sound go?

In the hallowed days of the trusty typewriter, scribes dealt with one of the most basic, yet complex, mechanisms ever created. Long before we sent out texts within hyper seconds, we composed letters and put them in the mail. And changing the ink usually meant getting a whole lot of it on your hands (and probably any white shirt you're wearing that day.)

The first typewriter I ever had was given to me by my Grandma Eva, in the mid-80s. I was about 11 years old at the time, and it was an antique model, a late 30's Remington 5 Portable. It was heavy and actually came in a wooden suitcase, so a secretary or salesperson could easily carry it with them wherever they would go.

It was also really cool-looking, and resembled all the ones I'd seen in old movies. The keys were round, and everything except the ribbon seemed like it was made out of metal. For a kid with a huge imagination, it was like pulling a literary sword from the stone.

The source of this gift, my grandmother, was an extraordinary woman and someone that I always looked up to for a number of reasons. She was incredibly learned and astute when it came to money, especially for the era she grew up in. At a time when most girls her age were being taught to focus on being housewives and homemakers, she was more adventurous and studious than that.

Perhaps that's why the little lady from a small town headed out west to attend college in Manhattan, Kansas. Once again, at a time when most girls her age - and from our area - didn't think on that grand a scale.

She was also a very kindhearted person, who saw the bigger picture when others often didn't. That led to her forging a lot of lifelong friendships and close ties in our community.

By the time I came along many years later, Eva had been married to my grandfather for years and was living back in Illinois. She became the Postmaster of our little town and was known for handing out Tootsie Roll Pops from behind the counter. If the little kids would 'act big' and be grown up enough to come in the office to pick up mail for their parents, my Grandma Eva would reward them with a sucker.

So, needless to say… it didn't take long before *every* kid in town was volunteering to go to The Post Office.

Trying to be really smart just like her, I practiced on that typewriter any time I was at her house. I would be just making stuff up and writing it. Silly skits or ideas for movies. Or, baseball statistics and sports stories. Anything that was on my little mind would end up on a piece of paper.

When I was little, the metal arms that hold the keys were really hard to push down. I was so small that my ring and pinkie fingers couldn't push them with enough force to make a dark imprint. So, I learned to 'type' with my other six digits: My index and middle fingers, and my two thumbs.

To this day, that's still how I do it - almost forty years later. I never changed, because it just became natural to me. All because of Grandma's old typewriter.

By the time I got to high school, she had basically given it to me, and I finally took it to my house for good. Let me tell you: I wrote a LOT of term papers on that thing. Later on, I used it for job applications and resumes.

And maybe even a few love letters to some girls, too.

Even now, with the ease of word processing, laptops, tablets and the like, it's hard not to miss that old Remington. I have always said one day that I wanted to buy the same model and replace it, but it still won't be the same.

There's just no replacing an original.
Just like there was no replacing my Grandmother.

What she gave me in life was much more than a typewriter. It was an extension of her life and her youth, passed on to me. She saw something special in me before I could ever see it in myself. And in many ways, it was the greatest gift I've ever received, because it enlightened me on what I wanted to become in this world someday.

My Grandma may have given me an outlet for my dreams in that wooden suitcase but she gave me something even more important, as well.

The belief that I could achieve them in my heart.

Thanks, Eva.

CHAPTER 1 | THE NOSE ALWAYS KNOWS...

"What is that smell? It's awful!"

We have five wonderful senses as human beings: Sight, Hearing, Touch, Taste, and Smell. The first few can all have unpleasant moments, but perhaps none of them accidentally betrays us more than that last one.

That's because you can control (for the most part) what you subject yourself to feel, taste, touch, see or hear... but you can't go without inhaling and exhaling.

Therefore, unless you can hold your breath like a deep-sea diver, you're going to get a sniff of some unwanted odors from time to time. And by 'unwanted', I mean to the point that they almost make you nauseous.

Most of these acidic aromas are the product of your fellow man. I'm sorry, but it's true. There are certain smells that people emit that are so powerfully pungent they could make an onion cry. They almost drive you to the point of losing all your faith in humanity.

You'll typically discover this somewhere like the gas station or your local dollar store. For some reason, there's always some trashy person lingering in the bread aisle who smells like a mix of armpit and anthrax. They're also usually the same people who like to wear a lot of tank tops in the summertime. The kind that really accentuates all their luxurious underarm hair. And that's just the women, for god's sake.

Riding in the car with your Dad is an experience that helps you understand exactly how gross another men's guts can truly be.

You may love your father and think he's a great guy. I know I certainly do; he's one of my biggest heroes in life was always there for me. My Dad truly is a role model and a person of principle.

But I have to warn you: You don't want to get caught in the car with the old man after a trip through the drive-thru at Taco Bell or White Castle.

Trust me, I've made that mistake a couple of times.
Doctors have told me that it may have taken 10 years off of my life.

Onions, skunks, rotten food, dead animals, and those sweaty socks you accidentally left under your bed last year, all produce some awfully evil air. Their foul fragrance can sometimes trigger post-traumatic stress disorder.

Of course, there's no need to complain about something we can't really snuff out. Unfortunately, it's a necessity to have a nose. Animals couldn't survive without it. After all, they use it to locate where they are, find food, and sniff people's crotches.

(I'm still not sure why dogs do that, but apparently it's a really big deal in the canine community. Word has gotten around.)

For humans, our sniffing ain't quite the same. However, we can still detect something rotten. Even when we're not in Denmark.

However? With any bad in life always comes much more good. There are those special smells that warm your heart and bring back wonderful memories. Some might even give you goosebumps or bring a tear to your eye.

It's the smell of Mom's home-cooked chili on a snowy day. And even though she told you to stay away from it until it's done, you can't help yourself. You have to sneak in and get a quick rush of the spices.

Ya know? Just to be nosy.

It could be the whiff of Fall weather when it's just starting to turn from hot to cool. It's a little bit of back-to-school breath or football fumes. And it represents a special time of year that will bring you back to your childhood, no matter how old you get.

It might be the steamy stench of the lake on a hot July day while fishing with your Dad. And eventually, your son.

Or just *maybe*... It's the scent of the girl you love. Her perfume, or whatever that sweet soap is that she uses. It's an air of tenderness and a gentle waft of acceptance. It's a scent you could get lost in forever.

Those are the smells that make all the intolerable ones tolerable. They make us appreciate all the things around us. They are the oxygen of our experiences on this Earth.

My suggestion is that you take in every aroma like any other experience. For better or worse? Life is out there. Breathe it in.

CHAPTER 2 | JUST WINGIN' IT

You may want to grab a few extra napkins for this one. It"ll probably get a little bit messy.

Around 50 years ago in Buffalo, New York, an unknown chef discovered where all the eternal mysteries of chicken lie. What happened next would change the landscape of culinary culture forever.

The buffalo wing was born, and cholesterol levels would never be the same. Ever since that day, we've been engaging in glorious gluttony... while licking our fingers the whole way.

Regular breading and basting suddenly become secondary to a meat preparation like we've never seen before. In fact someday, scholars may study this appetizing invention and measure it against other historic innovations like the wheel, the combustible engine, and the internet..

The buffalo wing, or 'hot wing', has become as much of a part of our culture as pot-bellies and foul flatulence. As a matter of fact, they're so popular that they should probably be considered a food group all by themselves.

Bathed in butter and cayenne pepper, these brutal babies can really leave a tangy taste on your tongue. That's because, while the basic framework may sound simple enough? A true wing-master knows it's all in the spice.

And with the right formula, those little chicken bits go great with any frosty, cold beverage of your choice.

As a society, we probably love wings because they're the most versatile finger food in the world. They can be served as an appetizer or the main course. They're delicious in Ranch, Blue Cheese, or all by themselves. They can be served breaded, or even naked as the day they were born. (Don't worry, it's our little secret.)

Everything from mildly mellow to hotter than hell is right there on the menu. People often say that variety is the spice of life. Over the years, the trusty wing has come dressed in everything from barbecue, lemon pepper, garlic, and honey mustard.

There's even a company that claims to have a chocolate-flavored chicken wing, but that sounds pretty fowl to me.

Here's another fine, feathered fact: Did you know that July 29th is Chicken Wing Day? Think about it like this: Millard Fillmore was our

13th President, and he doesn't even have <u>his</u> own holiday.

Wings are an MVP of the sporting world, also. It's estimated that during the week of the Super Bowl, about 160 million pounds of wings fly off the grocery store shelves.

Even people who aren't fans of the yard bird have to admit --- that's a whole LOT of poultry in motion.

A chain of very successful sports bars is named after them, so they're obviously a boost for the economy. As an added bonus, they also contribute to the paper towel and wet napkin industries, as well.

I used to be one of those macho guys when I placed my wing order. I would boldly tell the waitress that I wanted mine so hot that they would make the devil sweat: "Forget about the sauce; just put kerosene on mine and light a match. Burn, baby, burn!"

About fifteen minutes later, my stomach would feel like a churning volcano about to erupt. It forced me to see the error of my ways and I've turned things down a notch. These days, I savor the flavor, as well as avoid the perils of heartburn. See kids? With age, comes 'wings-perience'.

I suppose there are some folks out there who don't care for them. Maybe someone is a vegetarian, or doesn't like the spicy taste. That's understandable. But, the majority of folks I know are friends of the feather, and have a thing for the wing

So, what's the best way to eat them? A LOT. That's all that matters. The great thing about chicken wings is that they're one of those rare foods you can actually eat 20 of, and still somehow have room for pie.

When that quick bite to eat is over, you roll up your napkin and check your shirt for sauce stains. My guess is there are at least two of them. Wear them proudly.

For it makes no difference, wing eaters. You must continue on, manically munching away on mountainous amounts of those little morsels of meat.

And, trust me... No matter how many of those puny, little pinions you manage to polish off?

Absolutely NO ONE will have a bone to pick with you.

CHAPTER 3 | THE 'A'-TEAM

"A" is for apple. Like the kind you would give to your teacher.

But contrary to popular belief, the kids who bring red, delicious fruit to class every morning aren't necessarily the ones who get all the good grades. That spot is reserved for a very special few. Those handful of pupils - the ones who happen to hang out on the honor roll.

And while they always understand what's on the blackboard, there are many regular folks out there who don't quite understand them.

They are gifted. As in "A"... for accelerated.

There are the ones who stick out rather quickly. They start with shiny, gold stars on third grade tests and move all the way up to the dean's list in college. Often, while all other adolescents are still learning the alphabet, exceptional kids are already performing algebra.

Then, they go on to have an active social life - albeit not in the traditional sense. Smart kids spend their down time volunteering for clubs and activities, as do many of their (only) friends. They carry their books because they want to, NOT because they have to. You can usually find them winning spelling bees, certificates, and scholarships.

And believe it or not? They seem to enjoy being at the head of the class. Pretty weird, huh? I mean, seriously --- How strange do you have to be to actually *like* learning stuff?

Because of their penchant for answering questions that others can't, they're often shunned by their peers and made into outcasts. They find themselves closer to educators and mentors than they do the kids their own age. That often forces them to trade the joy of being a child for the seriousness of adulthood far too soon.

It's an odd mix of a thirst for knowledge, sprinkled with the price of success. Usually all occurring at a confusing time in one's life, unfortunately. Childhood and the teenage years are spent trying to fit in with the crowd. Being a celebrated scholar doesn't really allow for that.

It's kind of difficult, especially when they keep calling your name (over and over again) at the annual Scholastic Awards Banquet. Pretty soon, you get labeled with such creative adjectives as, 'nerd', 'dork', or 'teacher's pet'.

However, "A" also stands for 'academic' - and for a number of reasons.

Despite the countless wedgies of today, a 12-year-old wunderkind knows exactly where he's headed in life eventually. He's planning on attending a university that's wrapped in glorious green ivy. The only choice really comes down to becoming either a doctor or a lawyer. Then, a career in politics might come after.

Who knows? When you're young and brilliant, the game of Life can sometimes be mastered like it's Candy Land. It becomes simple and pliable, when a healthy dose of logic is applied.

After years of scholastic success, these brainiacs often become captains of industry or technological innovators. They are paid huge salaries to be supervisors, consultants, or advisors for major corporations around the globe.

Now suddenly? "A" stands for affluent.

Inventing the next great gizmo or travelling to space isn't just *cool*, it's also *profitable*.

A teenage genius has a really good chance at being a forty-something billionaire. In fact, it happens all the time in today's era of fast fortune and enormous income.

Brain power usually leads to financial success, especially for kids who are highly motivated. If they mix their intellect with the right "A"ttitude, they never run into any problems paying their bills.

What sets these wondrous minds apart is that they often accomplish all this while treated as strangers in a strange land. Despite all their talents, it's hard to solve the problem of loneliness. It just doesn't compute.

It's a shame, too. Instead of rewarding accomplishment, we seem afraid of it. We have an aversion. We're apathetic. And these amazing adolescents are often left abused or alone.

Maybe some day we will see the beauty behind such brilliant minds. In the meantime, the schoolyard A-Team can only hope for one more mark on the report card of life.

This time, they'd like another "A"... One that stands for 'acceptance'.

CHAPTER 4 | MAKING A MOCKERY OF MOVIES

Have you ever been watching a movie and sworn that you've seen it all before? Except, the setting was more intricate and the girl in the love scenes was a heck of a lot cuter. Oh yeah? The version you saw also didn't have a talking parakeet in it, either.

What does it all mean?
It means that it's 3 AM, and it's time to turn off your TV and go to sleep.

A 'mockbuster' is a slang term Hollywood observers have coined for a lower budget film that mimics a hit movie. This is obviously done in order to capitalize off the latter's success.

Most times, the plot, tagline, and title closely resemble that of the major motion picture that it's trying to piggyback off of. Unfortunately, the shortcomings are pretty obvious, resulting in what amounts to a bushel-full of rotten tomatoes.

These bastardized b-grade films are often either produced (poorly) for a basic cable network or are direct-to-rental offerings.

Keep in mind; these aren't remakes, reboots or spoofs. No, no, no. They're absolutely ripped from the real thing, right down to finding an alternate title by merely using a Thesaurus. Much like a pawn shop full of Rolexes, they're clearly knock-offs.

For example, when 'Alien vs Predator' originally debuted in 2004, it had the cash boxes ringing in theaters all over the world. And for good reason. It was the continuation of a valued and established franchise's storyline.

Needless to say, the 'Alien' fans out there were ready for this one long before it finally arrived on the silver screen. In fact, some of them even camped out for tickets to the premiere. That's happened many times with other blockbuster films in the past, as well.

Unfortunately, while Sigourney Weaver was battling beasts at your local bijou, her efforts were being matched at the same time by a smaller production named, 'Alien vs. Hunter'.

They were exactly, totally and completely the same film, except for the part about investing in really good actors and awesome special effects.

Unfortunately, some movie fans were duped by the intended confusion, and ended up renting the lesser film. They got home only to realize that they were victims of a classic bait-and-switch, Hollywood style.

Back in 1977, 'Star Wars' changed the history of film and pop culture forever. About a year later, a similar, yard-sale version of the same story was released.

It was titled, 'Star Crash'. Fittingly, it featured none other than David Hasselhoff, who - admittedly - has had a few crashes of his own over the years.

But mockbusters don't just happen in science fiction. They occur in the grown-up kind of movies, too.

For example, there's a steamy, erotica film called , 'Bound', that was released in 2015. There was only one problem: It was produced with barely half the budget of the movie it was was trying to copy.

In other words, it only had about **25** Shades of Gray in it.

It seems like every major motion picture has a doppelganger. Iron Man was countered by a similar looking, armored robot guy named Metal

Man. So as you can probably see, the creativity of a Hollywood producer isn't necessarily all the earth-shattering, after all.

Ironically, the mockbuster effect can strike families, as well.

While Laura Dern was starring in the wildly successful, smash hit, 'Jurassic Park', another lesser-known dinosaur flick was making the rounds in select theaters. Probably the kinds of places that were in seedy neighborhoods, or some single-screen setups that were attached to a bowling alley.

It was called 'Carnosaur', and it starred Dern's very own mother, Diane Ladd. Apparently in this case, blood money was thicker than actual blood, itself.

For every Pacific Rim you've got to have an Atlantic Rim. And if there's a high school musical, it's only right that there should be a movie about a Sunday school musical.

Or, a musical of any kind in some kind of environment where the main characters are being held down and oppressed. And all they want to do is put on a show, damn it. That's the whole plot. In all of them.

Unfortunately, this phenomenon happens more times than you can say, "Be Kind. Please Rewind."

Over the course of many years, these flimsy films were expected to be a substitute for a true hit. But in the end, they turned out to be something that only rhymes with the word, 'hit.'

It's a crying shame that the folks who make mockbusters are essentially cheating consumers out of their money by fooling them with an inferior product. It just makes everyone in Tinsel Town look really bad and reflects poorly on the entertainment industry. That just doesn't feel right.

Because after all, if you can't trust the people in Hollywood...
Who can you trust?

CHAPTER 5 | THINKING OUT LOUD

They say you shouldn't talk to yourself. It's a sure sign that you're going crazy.

We've all seen that person who comes wandering out of the grocery store or the bank, babbling something to themselves. They might be frustrated or giggling, but whatever is on their mind is uncontrollably popping out of their mouth.

Our usual reaction to this is to politely distance ourselves. And possibly look for the nearest police officer.

It's a strange sight, when someone's inner monologue just comes pouring out. And as much as we hate to admit it, we <u>all</u> do it every now and then. Our inner monologue often becomes outward without us even realizing it.

I honestly used to think My Father was losing it when he would walk through the house, muttering to himself and seemingly no one else. He would pass through a room, saying something about a missing screwdriver.

Then, he came back through a few minutes later, mumbling about the power bill.

It was like a confusing swirl of dad-speak.

At the time, I thought it was a little more than odd. Obviously, he had been bitten by a rabid dog or recently probed by aliens, because this behavior was not normal.

Whatever it was, it seemed like that codger was finally slipping off into the fifth dimension. We would probably have to call someone soon to have him taken away.

To my astonishment, the men in white coats never showed up. And he just kept on yapping for years.

My perspective changed, however, when I got older and found myself doing the exact, same thing.

Something I once laughed at became standard practice. After years of thinking those kind of people were all insane, I guess I must have checked into the asylum, too.

Going through my daily routine in life, I give myself verbal reminders all day long. In some form or the other, we all use this tactic, and it doesn't mean we're crazy.

It just means we're getting to the point where we need as many things to jog our memories as possible. For example:

Doctor's appointment at noon. Don't forget to call Mom.
Did I eat today?

Whether it's talking through where I've left my car keys, or asking myself what time the game starts, I find myself doing it more often these days. However, you eventually come to realize that those little chats we have with ourselves help us get through the day.

They also serve other purposes. Sometimes, you might have to push yourself through a tough workout:

Don't quit. You can do this.
Nothing can beat you.

Or, maybe you mouth to yourself that you shouldn't do something wrong. Perhaps you have to tell yourself aloud to do positive things. And if that's what works for you? Then by all means, keep babbling away.

You also might just do it as an emotional reflex, like reassurance when you're nervous or concerned. Especially if it's regarding something important that seems out of your control at the time:

Please let everything be okay. I hope my family's alright.

I've got to talk home.

Upon closer examination, the conversations we have with ourselves aren't really as crazy as one might imagine. Whether it's a reminder, encouragement, or just a laugh, those one-man chat sessions are just another quirky thing that gets us through life.

So, don't be afraid to talk to yourself.
It just might be the best conversation you ever have.

CHAPTER 6 | FISH STORY

Can someone please teach me how to fish?

I want to reel in a titanic trophy to mount on the wall in my office. Just so people actually think that I'm a capable fisherman. (When in actuality, I'm more likely to catch a cold instead of a carp.)

I realize it's not rocket science, but I just never seem to have any success at sea, and no luck on the lake.

Don't get me wrong, here. I understand the basics of it. The physical act of baiting, casting, and reeling, I got down pat. No problems there at all.

My question is: why can't I do the catching part? How does that little, finned menace keep finding a way to outsmart me and swim away every time? Because I have been to college, and I'm pretty sure he hasn't.

The last time I threw my line out in the water, I returned with an empty bucket. In fact? After investing $50 in supplies, I came back home with nothing more than a slight sunburn, a cut on my hand, and a really bad odor.

On my way home, I stopped to fuel up at the local gas station. That's when I overheard two old boys talking. One of them must have had a good day.

This guy clearly didn't spare the rod, at least based on his stories. And to hear him tell the tale? He had more fish than a Catholic church on a Friday.

I decided that I wanted to have stories like that. After hearing this wannabe Winkelman describing his Sunday adventures (which apparently involved battling fish that were on some kind of super steroids), I needed to be part of that club... funny hat, and all.

You know? The Fish Story Club. It hasn't been for lack of effort, either.

Just recently, I was out on the lake and used so much stink bait, you would have thought we were in the elephant tent at the zoo. I barely had my line in the water when it snapped. I swore I heard little fish laughter from a distance.

With my worm gone, I searched for the culprit. A blue gill swam by, and he immediately became a fish of interest.

I don't know why. Maybe it was because he just *smelled* suspicious.

I realize now that there is only one thing to do. These fish are clearly conspiring against me, so it's time to infiltrate them.

I have to completely focus on one thing, and one thing only... FISH. 24 hours a day. It will have to be a summer-long obsession.

So in preparation, I bought Carp coffee mugs, Pollock pajamas, and Walleye wall art.

An aluminum large-mouth bass happily accepts my mail from the postman every day. My clock is shaped like a Marlin, and it hums a wave of melodies by Muddy Waters.

They seem to be everywhere I look, too.

The other day, I was watching CNN and some guy was giving a speech on gay rights. The poster in the background reminded me of trout. Must have been all those rainbows.

Another time, I was sitting still in traffic for a few, annoying seconds. The light had already turned green, so I looked at the driver ahead of me.

It was a fish, with obviously nowhere to go and just out for the halibut. He was clearly not paying any attention.

I finally rolled down my window, threw up my arms, and angrily screamed, "GO, Fish!!!"

I don't know if I'll catch any this year, but I just keep going back for more. Until I can master the art of landing a whole mess of those sneaky swimmers, I'll be out on the lake every, single day.

Call it an aquatic obsession, but I refuse to cut bait.

No doubt about it... I'm hooked.

I'm sure the fish won't care either. They'll ignore whatever I write about them in this book and continue swimming through the waters of their day-to-day lives.

My musings won't stop their routine.
Heck, they probably don't even have time to read anything at all.

But if they do, they should at least take a closer look at a newspaper. They just might get wrapped up in it.

CHAPTER 7 | HEARD IT IN A LOVE SONG

They say that every song has a memory attached, and I believe that's true.

Whether you're streaming a jam from back when you were in high school, or listening back to your wedding theme on your 25th anniversary, there's a lot of rhythm that goes along with our remembrance.

It all comes back somehow, with just the beat of the rhythm of the night. You get lost in the lyrics and swept up in the soul. And the next thing you know, you're just a fool in love all over again.

Sometimes, when It's Been a Hard Day's Night, you just gotta Get the Groove Back. Other times? You're feeling so good that you're Walkin' on Sunshine or maybe even Dancing on the Ceiling.

With the flick of a radio dial, you can pretty much find the music to fit your mood. And no matter where your emotions lie, there's something about a romantic tune that will always pluck your heartstrings.

Maybe it's thinking about your first kiss after the Spring Dance or cruising down the street on the day you finally got your driver's license.

But - for a multitude of reasons - when a random number hits the airwaves, it can make your soul wander and your mind wonder. You get Hooked on a Feeling. The next thing you know, it's a lovely day for a Daydream, and Life is a Highway.

Then, there's the other side of the song spectrum.

Once, I watched a friend of mine literally break down in tears when we were driving together. The station slipped into a slow jam that reminded her of a long-lost love; she just couldn't hold in her feelings.

I didn't know the circumstances, but I tried to be understanding. Until then, I never knew that the Bee Gees could incite so much emotion.

In those situations, you're not really sure how to react. But I guess when they asked, 'How Deep Is Your Love?', it hit her so hard that she needed Too Much Heaven to lift her spirits.

One thing's for sure: The people who get paid to write those tear-jerkers must earn a fortune.

Just the right word or phrase seems to make us laugh and cry for the dumbest reasons. There's a whole swirl of emotions caught somewhere between Bon Jovi, Frank Sinatra, and Peabo Bryson.

In some ways, our favorite music is associated with who we were involved with at that time.

In other words, you can pretty much date a song based on who were dating at the time. We link the emotion in the lyrics with our own emotions at the time we originally heard them.

We also associate music closely with where we were in life. So it only makes sense that a melody can bring back a memory. Whether we want it to or not.

Whether you just received a Love TKO or you're belting out your Comeback Song, the inner workings of our brain react like a Pavlovian dog to these refrains. It's a funny way to reminisce about life, but it sure does seem to click in our minds.

However, sometimes there are other examples that aren't quite so silly. They aren't about falling down or getting up. These tunes hum a different kind of memory.

Maybe it's a song that reminds you of someone you have sadly lost. And it's a very different kind of love. Your Best Friend. Or, your Grandfather.

Then, you break down and cry. Turns out, our emotional attachment to music isn't so silly after all. At least, not when you put it into the proper perspective. It's just part of our makeup. It's the soundtrack of our soul.

So? Let Your Love Flow Like a Mountain Stream, and always remember: Let the Music Play.

CHAPTER 8 | POKING THE BEE HIVE

Listen up, honey.

It's getting warmer, and a favorite of the insect world is going to be making its rounds. As he flies through the air, no one is more delicate, yet dangerous, than the common bee.

Bees, scientifically classified as part of the Apoidea family, are a big part of our picnic and pool time. Noted for their ability to harvest nectar as well as give you a sudden sting, they attract your attention any time they're around.

While they can be dangerous, you shouldn't be allergic to the buzz around the bee community.

A hive can be very organized, mobilized, and 'pollin-ized' at any moment. Like an army of winged warriors, bees always seem to know their place within the colony.

One group. One mission. One identity.

People, on the other hand, are nothing like that. While we operate within a society, we often find our individuality makes it hard to be good, little soldiers.

So, as human beings, we come from all different types of swarms. Every individual is their own type of bee.

For example, if you listen to the 'used-to-bees', they will tell you how much better things were back in the day. They are always living for the past and complaining every time the world turns.

And maybe they're right. Growing up, we all remember watching our fathers holding down a job, fixing things around the house, or spending time with us.

In fact? Dad always seemed to be a real busy bee. And in the kitchen, there was my Mom... his honey bee.

Or, how about that young couple who finally decided to take the plunge? He just slipped a ring on her finger. They're not married yet, but they're part of a group called the 'about-to-bees'.

And the smell of the sweetness is everywhere. This spring, another group of wide-eyed graduates takes on the world. They are my favorite insects of all. They are the 'I'm-gonna-bees.'

Unfortunately, every rose also has its thorns. So on the flip side, there are also killer bees. The people who can manage to cause chaos among a field of daffodils and leave destruction in their wake.

For example, there are some men out there who think they're the type of bee that needs to pollinate as often as they can. They fly from flower to flower, cultivating as much as possible with no apologies.

Personally, I think they may be trying to compensate for the sadness in their stripes, or possibly the size of their stinger. We refer to those guys as 'wanna-bees.'

Or, what about the person who you are counting on to give you a ride, but you just know they are going to blow it? They always give you an EXTREMELY estimated time of arrival.

We call these people 'should-bees', because they are always letting you know when they "should be" there.

You've got those people that work out so much that they make you sick. Constantly in good shape, they make the rest of us look bad. I call them 'sweat bees'.

But every colony needs someone to follow. And the swirl of the family, the Queen is always the matriarch of the hive. Everyone else falls in line behind her.

We do things a little differently. We have no monarchy, and our society selects among our entire horde to find a leader. It's a big decision, too. We've got to swat the air, and somehow run safely to the right choice.

Sometimes, I think we might be better off if we were more like our friends, the bees. They live on instinct, and not emotion. They make no decisions for themselves, so they have no consequences for their actions.

We do. And that's what really stings.

CHAPTER 9 | PINE BOX DERBY

Have you ever heard the radio commercials that are offering you a chance to shop for your own funeral?

The ones where some guy that sounds like he's 185 years old starts talking to you about your 'eternal plans?' Even though it sounds like he might not make it through the whole advertisement?

They make it very easy for us deal with our own demise.
We can even pay for it now using PayPal.

The whole idea of this is just kind of weird and creepy when you think about it. And while I know that day will come, it's not really something I want to battle-plan for right now.

It's not that I have an absurd fear of death; I just think the post-rigor proceedings are a little morbid.

And while I realize the point is that you're taking care of your arrangements to spare your family the trouble, it's just bizarre to be window-shopping for it.

So, I guess I don't really have a problem with the point, but more in the way that it's presented.

For example, these places have package deals depending on how much you want to spend. Like a McDonald's extra value meal, the customer decides how super-sized they want their sendoff to be.

You get to pick your plot, clothing, the colors, music, and the most important accessory of all, the casket. Heaven's mattress.

That's right.
They're selling you death, and they even have a box for you to put it in.

But how do you pick out your casket? And more importantly, how much cash should you lay down for the place where you're going to lay down for eternity?

Another thing that makes it all baffling: We are encouraged to comparison shop for the prettiest tomb we can afford.

If you're already dead, do you really care if you're leaving on a golden plate... or in a piano crate? It's not like you're going to be posting a selfie of it on your Instagram account.

I'm not really all that picky, myself.

When you ship me out, you can use either paper or plastic. It makes no difference to me. At that point, I'm probably not going to be that worried about the environment that much, anyway.

During my call, the salesman kept giving details about his pimped-out pine boxes. One was even referred to as the 'Cadillac of caskets'. I guess that's because they *both* have something dead under their hood. (rim shot!)

The way they made it sound, everyone should get a burial that would make King Tut jealous.

Honestly, I think that says something about us as people. We want to be glorified in death, and we want to drive the sports car that gets us there in life. And when that lid finally closes, it's the last image the world has of us.

So it better be a pretty one, right?

I guess that's the appeal of shopping for your funeral. It symbolizes our own warped perception of our existence and place in the world.

Time and time again, we seem more concerned with surrounding ourselves with beauty in death, more than we do in life. Pretty creepy, huh?

CHAPTER 10 | LEGENDS OF THE FALL

I got up early the other morning and felt that certain, special chill in the air.

You know that chill. It's the early morning cup of coffee, get the kids on the school bus, "where's-my-sweater" kind of nip in the air. It's a symbol that it's about time to cozy up with Fall.

Or, Autumn. I'm not really sure.
And no one has clarified to me yet which term is more politically correct.

For all the years I have known the feel of the season, I've never really gauged it by the calendar. For me, it starts when I feel that dry, semi-cold morning that makes you start thinking of hay rides and homecomings.

I know what it means, and I love it.

I adore it, actually. I'm just not sure what to call it.

On one side you have the term, 'Fall'. It's one syllable and forcefully blunt. It's a reminder of the trauma of an upcoming winter.

After covering sports for so many years, fall also reminds me of football locker rooms that smell like spoiled sweat and cheeseburger farts. Oh, what beautiful memories.

Its doppelganger, 'Autumn', is two syllables and just sounds more pleasant. It's like the name of a pretty girl, standing in the September grass and smiling.

Just saying it sounds more melodic, like the chant of a Buddhist monk, or the words 'no money down'. It's all about laying in a hammock, curling up in a blanket, and sipping on a mug of hot, cocoa goodness.

So, I feel infatuated with both of them. I was raised to call it Fall, but I admit a slight flirtation with Autumn. They intrigue me in different ways. One is the strong, silent type. The other just seems so much more warm and comforting. It's like I can't pick between the two.

You see, I've learned my lesson.

I've been torn by two lovers before.

And for some reason, I always end up being the fall guy.

CHAPTER 11 | GIVING 'I DO' ITS JUST DUE

If you like it, then you really *should* put a ring on it.

Somewhere, in a field of daffodils, a family has gathered for a blessed day. Cue the music as the bride takes her father's arm. A few little tears trickle from her wet eyes.

A beautiful ceremony is sealed with a kiss, and then the newly-announced Mr. and Mrs. Whoever walks through a rainstorm of rice.

And in this one, glorious moment, they are a match made in heaven.

You've attended a million weddings before, but this is the *ONE*.
The couple rides off to a honeymoon in Vegas. Or, maybe even The Ozarks. They start a family, and they live happily ever after.

The End... right?

As we all know, it doesn't work that way. Despite all the time and trouble that goes into planning a wedding, the work that comes next is the hardest.

The true test of your love and affection comes when you have to start dodging someone else's sweaty socks or picking up their wet towels in the bathroom.

To hear the old folks tell it, those gold bands were what kept our little nuclear families from exploding. But as we grew up, our own experiences would shed some light on those myths about marriage.

Although I am happily married now, I've engaged in the pleasure of nuptials once before. That first effort didn't end so well.

Our experience wasn't very good for either of us, but we stuck through a lot of ugly times before finally giving up.

Like a round peg in a square hole, it was two people not meant to be, trying to hold on to what had become a meaningless pledge by that point.

Why? Because conventional society tells us that a wedding is an institution and divorce is a desecration. Moms and Dads should be married and then stay that way forever.

At least, that's the way the storybooks tell you it's always been.

In reality, people may talk a good game about marriage, but it appears to be a joke to most of them. The truth is that a good portion of our civil unions don't end quite so civil.

According to the website *mckinleyirvin.com*, a little over 41% of first marriages end in divorce, with the rate going even higher in the second or third. Also, the average length of a marriage that ends in divorce is just eight years. That's only long enough for two sets of Olympics!

Celebrities have also done their part to piss on the concept of matrimony. Sometimes they marry for publicity; sometimes it's for money. Britney Spears got hitched once for a total of 55 hours before calling it quits.

Can you believe that? Some people rent cars. She rented a husband. Even Elizabeth Taylor had to be impressed.

It seems as though monogamy is almost illegal in Hollywood. And now, we have a slew of reality TV shows that have turned marriage into a meat market for those merely trying to become celebrities.

Perhaps marriage is most relevant when it comes to legal or financial issues. Quite simply, people who are married receive benefits that single people don't. Family plans, discounts, and insurance rates may be made available to you, thanks to the fact that you have a spouse.

So starting with the license itself, marriage in today's society can sometimes look like nothing more than one, long paper trail.

At the end of the day, maybe there isn't any emotion left anymore, and it's all just a business arrangement wrapped in roses and lace. That may be a bit of a cynical view, but it's also somewhat accurate.

This is not to downplay anyone's wedding vows. I understand that different people have different values, and some couples have terrific marriages.

However in many cases, it can typically be a no-win situation.

Why in the world would someone want to take that chance on another person? Who wants to worry about potentially spending years banging their head against the wall over whether or not the meat loaf was good?

In the relationships that truly work, love and affection can trump all the paperwork, the statistics, and the odds. People still blindly go with their heart, hoping for the best. The ones who are successful are the ones who use their head enough to deftly dodge divorce.

And that's why it survives, despite being so battle-tested.

Marriage lives on because we all have that feeling in our gut that out of all those millions of weddings, ours really will be the *one*.

We have the right to feel that way, too. There's no shame in believing in some sort of stability in this ever-shaky world. The feeling that there's one person out there for you - and that you want to go through a ceremony to prove it - is something everyone can happily dream about.

No matter what the numbers say, I am 100% behind the folks out there taking that shot. I hold on to the idea that the sanctity of marriage can evolve in this changing world, and happy couples will never go extinct.

The world may change, but the concept of matrimony, co-habitation, and family will live forever.

So despite all the bad news you see out there, I still believe in marriage.

For you. And me. And **everybody**.

CHAPTER 12 | TAKE IT EASY, GREASY

It's time for an oil check.

There's a certain freedom about having the keys to a car in your hands. You know you can fire it up, put that thing in drive, and go just about anywhere that the rubber meets the road.

At work or at play, you love your ride, because our four-wheeled friends get us to our destination without fail, *most of the time.*

Inevitably, however, there comes a point when your trusty Toyota or venerable Volkswagen begins to wear down. After a while, it begins to hide its age worse than Kenny Rogers did.

Suddenly, there's a sound coming from somewhere under the hood. And not the normal, 'vroom-vroom' sound.

It's either a knock or a rub, or maybe a knock that's causing a rub. All you know is that you don't know, and need the opinions of an expert. That's when you get to deal with your local auto mechanic.

He comes strolling out in a half-buttoned shirt with his name patch on it. There's a gob of grease on his fingers and he's sporting the kind of mustache that would make the Mario Brothers envious.

His accent is part-Cajun, part rocket science, and he mumbles something about worn belts and stripped tires. Or maybe it's stripped belts and worn tires. You don't understand anything he's talking about, but you're pretty sure it's going to cost you a ton of money.

As you leave your keys at the counter, you're left with the thought of your car being in the dirty hands of this so-called 'automotive technician.'

Hopefully, you've cleared out any personal items regarding your religion, sex life, or net worth. (Because trust me, he's definitely going to go through your shit.)

The time it takes for the service seems to take forever, too. Soap operas play on the waiting room television. You spend what feels like an eternity thumbing through old magazines and drinking lukewarm coffee.

Pretty soon, it becomes apparent that these guys really DO get paid by the hour.

But, there are alternatives.

I've had a few 'shade tree mechanics' work on my car over the years.

You know the guy I'm talking about. He works in his backyard or a cousin's garage. And he's the kind of dude who will fix your transmission in exchange for a six-pack and a carton of cigarettes.

However, you might also run across one who will sell your muffler to buy meth. So, as always, buyer beware.

As far as most mainstream shops go now, they have a lot better code of ethics than the good, 'oiled' days. The training is much more advanced, the equipment is more technical, and customer service people typically communicate better with their wary consumers.

But, the old stereotype still exists. We all have awkward anxiety when we hear a sound or feel a vibration while driving. Because we know we might soon be getting some bad news about our car's condition.

What if it's worse than you thought? What if your vehicle is completely shot? You really need and love your car. Now, its destiny is in the dark, busted-up hands of your mechanic.

A momentary shock rushes through you and your wallet. You begin to wonder how you're going to get out of this potentially time-consuming and (therefore) costly situation.

That's when he looks you in the eye, smiles, and says, "It was just a small, pin-sized leak. No big deal. You're all set and ready to roll."

"By the way, that'll be fifty bucks."

CHAPTER 13 | BRUSHING OFF HEARTACHE

It's better to have loved and lost, even if you end up losing a little of yourself. At least that's what the brokenhearted always try and tell themselves.

For anyone who has ever come out of a long, serious relationship, there's an awkward phenomenon that follows. It's sort of like a galactic grace period in life.

Be it silent, stressed, or sorrowful, the feeling that follows always seems to have something in common: The impulse inside that something you once had is missing.

It may not be emotional. It may not be financial. But like that old song says... every time they go, they take a piece of you.

Because we are creatures of habit, we often have to alter our behaviors when we have a mate. It may be something as small as getting used to their spare toothbrush being over at your house.

It will be right there, hanging next to yours, to the point that they will be almost touching. Pretty gross, huh?

After some time, though, you learn to accept that brush and the germs that might potentially come along with it. You learn to push it to the side and just make some room for yours.

Eventually, they each have their own, color-coded bristle covers. One happily hygienic family is born.

In this case, you don't mind giving up a little of your comfort, and some of your bathroom real estate, for the one you love. It seems small, but it's very symbolic.

From there, we begin to sacrifice our time, our likes, and our friends - often slowly and gradually. Our better half does, too, as you begin to intertwine around one another.

Their habits become yours, and each of you begins to take on the other's traits. Finishing each other's sentences becomes almost commonplace. In extreme cases, some couples even spend so much time together that they even start to look a little bit alike.

When romance reaches that level, it typically goes one of two ways. In one scenario, those soulmates stay together forever, spending the rest of their lives deciding on whether to have chicken or fish for dinner.

But when "goodbye" is the only way things can end, there's always a feeling of weirdness for awhile. That surge of regret mixed with angst is somewhere deep inside, and it feels like it's never going to go away.

Even though things might be over, there's still no closure there. Because deep inside, you already know what tomorrow is going to bring:

No more silly habits and funny discussions. No more laughing or crying. No more toothbrush.

And that's the sad part. Every mile you walk away from someone still can't replace what you leave behind. It feels like something is escaping you. So even if that person is no longer part of your heart, they are still a part of your history.

That's why a broken heart is often just like a cavity.
It leaves a hole inside that you just can't brush away.

CHAPTER 14 | SLITHER ME TIMBERS

I guess it's a bit of a cliche to say that April showers bring May flowers. Everybody knows that already. They've even written it in books and such.

But among all the greenery, there's an especially creepy character who also comes out to stretch his belly in the Spring sunshine.

He once started his journey in The Garden of Eden. But today, he's made his way into The Garden of You.

Welcome to the season of the snake. Keep your shovels, spades, and (possibly even) machine guns ready.

There's something about this rope-shaped reptile that has not only fascinates us, but at the same time, scare the bejesus out of us.

I won't begin to discuss all the biblical connotations or political imagery that a serpent evokes. When it comes to pop culture and history, there's no denying their standing. Even though, *technically speaking*, they don't even stand at all.

I'm not talking about that big bastard in 'Anaconda', either.

I mean your average, everyday snake. The ones who think it's cool to hide under a potted plant, on a patio rug, or in my sock drawer. They're real wise guys like that.

You know what I'm talking about. Because of their size, color, and shape, a snake can often move undetected and easily hide from our human eyes. This natural-born camouflage is another thing that's calculating about these creatures of deception.

Like a slasher in a horror film, they're just waiting to pop out and frighten the hell out of you. Then, that instant moment of panic usually reminds you that you drank too much Pepsi earlier that day.

I'm sure, at least once, everyone has grabbed a stick, cable or hose that turned out to be moving. My mother accidentally 'discovered' a snake like this once.

To this day, she still holds the world record in the high jump (and she was 63 years old at the time.)

With their beady eyes, whip-like tongues, and unforgiving visages, they make a perfect villain. They're like the Darth Vader of the backyard, complete with that same, scary hissing sound.

In fact, snakes are so cunning, I heard they even tried to hijack a plane once. It's true; they made a movie about it.

They can move like a ninja, yet strike like a samurai. Their unexpected visits can ruin an afternoon tending to your tomatoes or a morning walk to get the paper.

I believe it's that type of uncertainty that gives so many folks a phobia of snakes. It's the thought that you can be totally relaxed and comfortable one minute, and terrified the next.

Just like lounging in your beach chair can be suddenly interrupted by a quivering interloper, life also gets tilted by a lot of other unknowns.

I think our irrational fear of a relatively harmless animal reflects our need to always have a handle on the situation around us.

It's almost a metaphor for having control. We just don't like the idea that something we fear can pop up at any given minute, leaving us defenseless and afraid.

Unfortunately, neither snakes nor uncertainty are going to be extinct any time soon. Both will be somewhere, lurking. They will always be there to scare you, and remind you that you can never enjoy your time in the sun too much.

There's only one thing we can do. Keep our eyes open and make sure that they don't jump up and bite us on the... WATCH OUT!

CHAPTER 15 | FORTY OUNCES TO FUNNY

"He's a happy drunk."

That's a common expression people use to explain when someone can tolerate their liquor without getting too aggressive. It's a funny way of saying that you enjoy sharing a beverage or two with someone, because they remain relaxed when they're inebriated.

Most of the time, these types of folks are really jovial and the life of the party. They've always got some recycled, old jokes that get a cheap laugh. And, they're always happy to take a free round from someone who they've made chuckle.

For the most part, they get a little sloshed, but they're essentially harmless. They just want to have a good time and keep the party going, which is pretty easy to do.

I should know, because I was a happy drunk for years. Or maybe I should say... that's what I always *thought* I was.

For the most part, I got along with everyone at my local bars and hangouts. Of course, over the years, you're likely going to run into some random redneck who wants to start a fight.

But if you frequent the same place, most of the regulars will run those mouthy morons off. Somewhat out of loyalty. But mostly, just to keep an outsider from upsetting their little apple cart.

I was one of those people who knew everybody. If you and I hadn't had a drink together, then you were either a teetotaler or just plain boring.

And I didn't have time for all that. I was too busy acting crazy and drinking myself into attempting any dare that my friends would throw my way.

Trust me, I did a lot of crazy shit when I was swimming in booze. I drove fast, talked trash, and showed my ass. Sometimes *literally*.

I liked a lot of excitement, action, and quick interaction. A 'hi', a laugh, and a hug. Then, it was off for another drink and more laughs elsewhere.

Was it fake and/or phony? Sure. But so is everyone else in that environment. Taverns aren't typically touted as temples of truth.

We're all just a lot of people in a stuffy tavern, with red cheeks, a lot of regret, and half-spilled drinks.

As the music fades out, the laughs die down, and everyone runs out of good jokes. There's a duller vibe and a deep lull sets in. Even a 'happy drunk' can't lift anyone's spirits.

Believe me, I've tried several times in the past. But people just grew more surly when all I wanted was to lighten the mood.

That's when the happy drunk slinks to the end of the bar, alone. In my case, I would make sure to polish off a couple more beers as quietly as I could.

Then, I packed up what was left of my soul and hoped that I wouldn't get pulled over on my way home.

Once I got there, I'd sit and listen to quiet music, sipping down what was left of the night. All alone, in the near dark, I usually came to realize one thing: The term 'happy drunk' is absurd.

Because there is no such thing as a happy drunk.

It's just someone who is trying to use alcohol to smile at their suffering.

— At least, I know I was.

CHAPTER 16 | GIVE ME A JINGLE SOMETIME

I've got a song that I'd like to teach the world to sing.

Throughout the course of a day, some funny thoughts float across your brain. Between work schedules, grocery lists, and appointments, a lot of things take up real estate in our grey matter.

Sometimes, you may tune into some TV to take your mind off things and guide you through the paces of life. It usually provides some musical clues on what your next move should be.

TV will let you know when you need to head for the mountains, have it your way, or deserve a break today. It reminds you that while you may be a Pepper, you also sometimes feel like a nut.

Welcome to the world of commercial jingles.

They will annoy you with their silliness, while at the same time hypnotizing you into purchasing their products. No doubt about it, a song from an advertisement can both entertain and entice us.

I fall into the trap of those little tunes, just like everyone else does. I could be getting dressed or making a sandwich, and a mishmash of commercials involuntarily floats through my subconsciousness.

That must be why they call them 'brands'. Because their themes are always branded in our brains.

It's true. I might just be walking around and suddenly, for some reason? I don't want to grow up, and I feel fresh and full of life.

Then, I head into the kitchen for a little plop-plop, fizz-fizz. I had developed a headache, because the damn cat kept going, "meow meow meow meow meow" all night long. It certainly wasn't the best part of waking up.

I adjust the thermostat, because it's getting chilly on my baby back ribs. I start making some warm soup, because (as we all know) soup is good food.

Suddenly, someone reaches out and touches me. It was a telemarketer, and I could tell right away that she was full of B-O-L-O-G-N-A.

Those are just a few examples of how commercialized music gets to us.

It binds an ordinary product with a catchy tune in an effort to grab our attention and money.

It works, too. For example, I'm not sure if Rice-a-Roni really is the 'San Francisco treat' or not, but it doesn't matter. My brain thinks it is, due to the rhythmic repetition it associates with that particular pasta.

Because of these tactical tunes, we now know that a Mazda goes zoom-zoom and foot-longs are only five dollars.

Those are a couple of more modern examples. But in the past, we were reminded to Have a Coke and a Smile, or sip on the Choice of a New Generation. Those songs kept playing with a message that resonates for more generations to come.

Those catchy little numbers, in their own way, are the salt on top of our two all-beef patties. They add just enough identity to their products that they convince us that certain things are better than others. Before you know it, you're tasting the rainbow and riding the ship that sails the ocean.

(And, If you've ever been a college student in Carbondale, Illinois, you can probably still remember the number to Quattro's Pizza.)

Thanks for reading. And just for the record, this chapter of the book has been brought to you... *by Mennen*!

CHAPTER 17 | BOYS DON'T CRY

It's time to man up.

As young guys, we are taught a lot of things in the process of growing up. Much like shaving and learning to curse, every boy is clued into the things that will make them as masculine as they're *supposed* to be.

There are certain unwritten rules you have to follow to be in the club. No girls allowed, of course.

For example: Never show weakness. Never be afraid.

And for goodness sake, son, don't ever let them see you cry. After all, that's what wimps do.

We've come a long way in society when it comes to breaking social stereotypes, but this isn't one of them. It seemingly applies to all males.

Some of the most truly admired men in the world have been openly heckled for showing their soft side. It's just goes against all the machismo ever displayed by our existence on Earth.

Even the typical catchphrases that guys use are hardcore:
Kill or be killed. I feel the need for speed. Die hard. (And, after a few more years) Die Harder - the sequel.

If you listen to guys tell their war stories, they're all robotic killing machines who can drink 15 gallons of beer, hold down three jobs, and have both a wife and a mistress at the same time.

If they break an arm at work, it's no problem. They just re-set it, and then work an overtime shift, because things would never get done without them.

Yeah, that's right. MEN. They're tougher than old shoe leather, baby.

That's why guys aren't supposed to show their sensitive side. It's an unwritten rule that men will do anything to avoid emotions. They're more likely to do cool, destructive stuff like blowing up mailboxes or shooting their friend in the butt with a dart gun.

Or if men start really getting too far into their feelings, there's always a huge batch of liquor nearby to quickly drown them away.

But, it's not always like that.

Sometimes, we have to stop being as rugged as an overcooked steak, and be a little more tender in the middle. So at certain points in your life, it's okay to shed a manly tear or two.

And I'm not talking about for stupid stuff, either. For example, if you cried because your favorite player was traded to another team, that doesn't warrant any waterworks.

Knowing his lifetime batting average can't qualify as true, emotional attachment. And, catching that foul ball during the playoffs doesn't count, either.

Also, you can't include any time your eyes might water when you're lifting weights or doing any other strenuous activity. That's simply a physical reflex. So, we'll just call those 'testosterone tears'.

I'm talking about the times that really matter. That's when you get a free pass for folding up. Like seeing your son being born, or even watching him march off to war. Mourning the loss of a wife or praying for a sick child.

Or maybe, it was the feeling in your stomach when you heard the National Anthem for the first time after 9/11.

When something like that hits you in the gut, it starts moving north pretty fast. Pretty soon, it's a huge lump in your throat that turns into uncontrollable water coming from your eyes.

Quite frankly, I don't think that makes anyone a lesser man. As a matter of fact, I think it makes them MORE of one.

There's no shame in actually showing that you care about something more than you do yourself. Vanity only goes so far in some situations, and true matters of the heart aren't one of them.

When my grandmother died, I tried to hold all of that kind of stuff in. She not only helped raise me, but she was also probably the most inspirational person in my life.

As I delivered a speech at her service, I felt it coming. I had held on to that stress too tightly, and now, I was shaking and sick to my stomach.

So, sometimes, it's better to just let the bad stuff out.

We all do it anyway, no matter what facade we hide behind. It's no secret that everyone has a soft spot somewhere near their heart that has nothing to do with cholesterol.

But, for some reason, we seem to find it funny or wimpy when another guy openly weeps. Which sure seems a tad hypocritical, considering there isn't a man alive out there who can say he's never broken down before.

Because as much as we may want to deny it? Sometimes our feelings take precedent over our facades.

That's why I won't do it anymore. Through all my ups and downs in life, I've learned to never laugh at a man who's crying.

Especially if that man is the one in the mirror.

CHAPTER 18 | A STATELY AFFAIR

Fluff your bonnets and load up the wagon. We're headed to a wingding.

It's just about fair time for all of us country folk. You can even call them picnics or carnivals if you like, we don't mind.

Your city, village, or province won't matter either. Just assemble all your friends and neighbors for a gathering of local fellowship - and some bingo.

Pass those waffle cones and giant turkey legs.
It's the perfect weekend for puttin' ribbons on hogs and mustard on dogs.

From childhood to our adult years, we all enjoy the festivities of our local fair. At some point during the summer, a fascinating troupe of folks sets up camp in town to entertain us. We watch for two days as they assemble a glowing village of wonder at our local park.

It's time to alert the children. A smaller, more hillbilly version of Disney World just arrived in our little hamlet. At a frantic pace, the locals scrape up cash for fair passes. They need a ticket to ride, and they don't care.

As you approach that first night of magic, the smell of fried dough fills the air. Kids pair up and decide about what rides to go on first. Parents talk about local politics while they congregate at the beer tent.

Off in the distance, a guy with a bushy beard, a bandanna, and a biker vest is setting up the ring toss game. His sign says 'NO REFUNDS', and it looks like he means it.

The good, kind citizens enter through the park like Christians being released to the lions. At first, they look a little confused, as if they've been locked in the trunk of a car for a few hours.

But eventually, they become comfortable and fall in line.

Soon, they will spend lots of their hard-earned cash on a night of down-home debauchery. It's the same money that the carnival folk will later use to invest in vodka, toilet paper, and Spaghetti-O's.

They say the only difference between a cab driver and a limo driver is that one of them wears a suit. If that's true, then the only difference between a carny and an astronaut must be an actual diploma.

After all, these guys appear to be pretty skilled. They can actually run The Scrambler and still smoke a Marlboro Red at the same time.

Forsaking any logic, you can't wait to jump aboard. The roller coaster operator stands there like Dr. Kevorkian, asking you if you're absolutely SURE you want to try out his machine of death. You seal a demonic pact with him and climb onboard.

About ten minutes later, you step off a rocking carriage, walk a few feet, and throw up.

Suddenly, that four-dollar chocolate shake doesn't seem like such a good idea anymore.

Meanwhile in the background, the faint sound of 'Peggy Sue' plays. A baby cries in the distance. Then, a woman screams at said baby.

Before you know it, over two sweaty hours have elapsed. The rides have been ridden, and you feel like you've been in the middle of a war zone. All you have left is two dollars in change and the kazoo that you won by shooting water into a clown's mouth.

Inevitably, the night starts to wind down and so do the patrons. The roller coasters stop, and some of the lights begin to go dark.

The last drunk staggers off into the shadows - with the help of a buddy who's just as wasted as he is.

A little girl cries over a toy that just broke.
The one her Dad just spent 40 dollars to win.

It's a kaleidoscope of craziness. But for a short and strange span, an entire community comes together as one. As silly as it might sound, we all kind of like those warm nights and that frozen lemonade.

The thought of backyard bingo and pageant princesses may sound silly to some, but not to the people who wait for it every summer.

We love to ring the bell with our sledgehammer and jump in our socks around the bouncy house. And, we just can't wait for the fried chicken and custard pie.

It gives people in a small town something to look forward to. So, in many ways, our annual summer fair is a great tradition. It swirls us together in a mix of fun, folklore, and funnel cake.

Having said that?

Thank goodness it only happens *once* a year. I don't think our little town could take too much more excitement than that.

CHAPTER 19 | MIRROR, MIRROR

Rise and shine. Smell the coffee.

It's a blessing just to wake up every day, isn't it? The sun shines through your window like honey dripping from the sky. You stretch and yawn, thanking all those lucky stars who helped you make it through another restful night.

Right after you give credit to your maker for another glorious dawn, it's now time to meet your judgement. As you stumble your way to the bathroom, an old friend is waiting to greet you: the morning mirror.

This is the time in your life that you might feel your worst.

Between the bad breath and the bed head, you realize that both you and your reflection should NOT be seen in public like this.

Everyone has their own morning rituals: the brushing of the teeth, the washing of the face, and even the scratching of the ass. If you are feeling particularly aggressive, you may even do some leg stretches with your foot propped on the toilet.

Whatever gets your blood flowing and your java percolating. It's time to face the world; you better be ready.

That's about when you begin to notice all of your flaws.

Maybe it's a pimple. Or, your hair isn't quite right, and you've been putting off getting your teeth cleaned. Your favorite shirt is creased, and you probably need to lose a few pounds.

It's all right there. Your faults are staring right back at you, and you just *know* that everyone else will see them, too.

Scars, boils, bruises, and wrinkles are there on display. Gray hair and bloodshot eyes don't help much either.

I've had those terrifying moments myself. There have been plenty of mornings when I didn't want to take a good look at my own face. As a matter of fact, I stood at the bathroom sink and swore I was in a fun house.

Not every day is brutal, however. Over the years, I have found that every mirror can be sort of 'double-sided' in its own way. Once in a while, we get a glance at something we didn't quite expect. We look into our own eyes and actually *like* what's there staring back.

Sometimes, you just have to stop and holler and pop your collar. You've got on the right jacket and tie, and you're ready for a night on the town. Or, maybe it's prom night, and you look like a princess.

Everyone has those times when they stare into the glass and see reflection perfection. It's an incredible moment when you're sexy, and (quite frankly) you know it.

At that point, we face up to ourselves, and we realize there is a lot more there than just a flat facade. That depth is what reminds us that we can walk out of the door and face the world. And, it's all right there, looking back at us - like the truth often does.

That's the funny thing about mirrors. They tell both sides of the story.

Sometimes, the person you see looking back is the person you hate the most. Other times, it's the one you love.

It's all a matter of your own opinion. So, I guess it all depends on how you reflect on things.

CHAPTER 20 | 'IT' HAPPENS

'Some guys have all the luck.' - Rod Stewart

There's no denying it, there are some special people out there in the world. Whether it's a prodigy or a superman, there are just some folks who just seem destined for greatness. The chosen ones are pretty easy to spot.

Then, there are those <u>other</u> successful people. The ones that you can't quite figure out. Call it dumb luck or perfect timing, but many men stumbled upon success simply by tripping their way forward.

You know the type: He may appear to be an Average Joe, yet somehow he's dating a lovely prom queen. Or, he's the guy with basic intelligence who amazingly gets voted Most-Likely-To-Succeed.

He's the placekicker who becomes the team MVP, or the McDonald's employee who motors around in a Mercedes. Somehow and some way, these dudes find a way to be normally abnormal. And vice versa.

Say hello to the IT Factor.

A now legendary term, it often describes people who - for no obvious or clearly discernible reason, find amazing success.

They don't necessarily have outstanding looks, smarts, style, or (in some rather extreme cases) hygiene. But for some reason, they're always magically walking between the raindrops. Meanwhile the rest of us are getting soaked.

Essentially, these people are the lottery winners in the game of life. Lyle Lovett would be proud.

I guess it's true what they say: Everyone has something that makes them attractive to at least a handful of folks. But these guys seem to have special traits that the whole world adores.

Whether it's a combination of wit and a winning smile, or aggressiveness and good timing, there are certain men who carry themselves above all others.

Maybe it's his handshake or his walk. Maybe it's the way he speaks or smiles. But for some reason, people flock to to the fella with the flow.

And quite frankly, it's an amazing gift to have. A guy with "it" doesn't wait for a table at a restaurant; he makes friends with the waiter and takes a seat. Good Old Mr. Wonderful always gets the best deal on a car. When he leaves the restroom, he never gets toilet paper stuck to his shoe.

And despite being the biggest, bitchiest brat in the whole family, he's still his mother's favorite.

He walks into a bar as a stranger, and leaves everyone's new best friend. People buy him a drink and offer him a cigar. And, they don't even mind that he's putting his hand in their pocket while he's patting them on the back.

A guy like that can go anywhere. From the bottom of the sea to the top of the mountain. From the north pole to the south pole. Or, from New York to LA, armed with just his aura.

When you're full of "it", you can do anything.

Like, be President.

CHAPTER 21 | NO MORE PLAYIN' AROUND

Ready, player one?

Dropping a quarter into the slot of a video game was a guilty pleasure for many of us as kids. It was a combination of sights, sound, and skill that we had never experienced before.

The people in my age group, commonly referred to as Generation X, were the first to widely enjoy this new form of entertainment.

Needless to say, we fell in love with it at first click.

In the early 80's, arcades provided scores of smiles and also collected millions of quarters in the process. A dark refuge for underage adventurers, Mom or Dad would often drop us off with a pocketful of change.

After punching the start button, we began maneuvering towards a 9-year-old's dream of achieving the high score on Bubble Bobble.

Minutes, sometimes hours, would pass. With your shoes stuck to a floor full of spilled Dr. Pepper, you wiggled behind a mystifying wooden box.

Your knuckles were white, and the smell of nacho cheese was in the air. Beeps, bops, and bells emitted from that space-age machine, while we tried collect the most points or save the universe.

Locked into the action like the pieces in Tetris, we left our world to engage in War Games or go on a Jungle Hunt. Adolescents were lined up at every machine, one right after the other, just like a Centipede.

Try as you might, you couldn't even Scramble away from the chaos. And since we couldn't Out Run the madness of the arcade, we all just went Berserk!

Every game had some sort of quest or goal to achieve. Often, we would Joust the top spot on the scoreboard, just so we could act like a Commando at school the next day.

Unfortunately, the competition could often get ugly, as some of the more aggressive gamers clearly had Xevious intentions.

That happened a lot more than you might think. Once back in '82, a riot broke out at a Frogger tournament. I wasn't there, but I heard that somebody got jumped.

Victory could sometimes be hard to accomplish, however, because there was always some nefarious character out to stop you. Between scorpions or snakes, aliens or animals, every world had some kind of digital danger waiting at the next level.

Every now and then, we had to rest our fingers, eyes and brain. So, we headed over to the concession area for a little bit of Burger Time. There, we got a lukewarm lunch for three bucks. Paid for in quarters, of course.

After escaping a Dragon's Lair and running the Gauntlet, you might get promoted to a spot in Missile Command.

Or perhaps you like manual labor. Then, may I suggest you put in some overtime in a game of Dig Dug?

You might've even taken a seat and grabbed the steering wheel in the Pole Position. (After all, *every* child needs driving lessons.)

The arcade era was truly a social phenomenon. Pac-Man and Donkey Kong became cultural heroes, immortalized on TV shows, comic books, Trapper Keepers, and Happy Meals. The incredible electronic boom of the 80's thrilled us, and the general public demanded more.

Realistic graphics and intricate game play replaced the simple wooden cabinets of our youth. Improvements and accessibility powered up those little kids' games, turning them into a mass-produced, trillion dollar industry.

With that, the children of the emporium became teenagers and subsequently moved the laser beams to their living rooms. Before we knew it, the good old arcade became a thing of the past, as we put the game in our homes and our hands.

In a way, it's a little bit sad. I drove past an arcade the other day, and there were no more flashing lights or kids buying tokens.

Galaga was gone. Defender had been ditched. Broken-out windows replaced Breakout, and the plumbing was leaking so badly that even Mario couldn't fix it.

Those classic games are still around, although in a newer, much fancier form. And while it's still a lot of fun to fire up some Q-Bert on your big screen or your iPhone, it's just not quite the same as the old days.

Sadly, the local arcade is a fad that seems to have faded. It's passing also wistfully reminds me that my childhood is long gone, too.

Unfortunately, they've both fallen victim to the two words that we never wanted to hear as kids: <u>Game Over</u>.

CHAPTER 22 | GET YOUR MOTOR RUNNIN'...

Check your mirrors. Then, put it in drive and crank it up. There's only one way to go when it's time to roll. There has to be a little music in the background when you put some rubber to the road.

Whether you used to push in an 8-track or rewind your favorite cassette, every good journey deserves a soundtrack.

It's a documented fact that driving - in and of itself - is rather boring. It's tedious and annoying at times. One cure to this dilemma is a little bit of mood music.

I suppose it's not a good idea to take your attention away from high-speed traffic just because Zeppelin came on the radio, but we do it anyway.

I often wonder how many deer have been accidentally hit by guys who just *had* to close their eyes while they play the air guitar solo.

It can be as Kool as Moe Dee or as Weird as Al, but for some reason it just sets the mood for a car ride. Miles of highway have been traveled, singing along at the top of our lungs with Bobby McGee.

It's not all positive, however. Our traveling tunes can sometimes be a source of contention. I know some people who get agitated if you change the station. Seriously. They will throw you out of their car. While its moving.

On the bright side, music can even get you through gridlock on the open road. There's nothing like a little 'Baby Got Back' when traffic is backed up.

There are times when the passing lane is moving so slow, we wish we could just walk 500 miles. Here's a tip: Next time, you might want to take a Big Yellow Taxi down that Freeway of Love.

For example, no matter what your taste for the race, you gotta put some metal behind your pedal. A little KISS or shock of AC/DC can really set the mood.

Sure, you may be driving a station wagon that is spray painted three different colors, but it's cool. With just the push of a button, you can instantly be 'Back in Black', baby!

Or maybe your taste is more gangsta.
And as we all know, bumping a little bit of hip-hop as you roll through the suburbs sends a message. It let's people know that you are one bad apple, and you shouldn't be picked at.

Even the biggest idiot in the world gets those precious few minutes to refer to himself by the name 'Big Poppa'. And when he does, he always remembers to represent his peeps.

The great Tom Cochrane once sang that life is a highway. Sadly years later, the not-so-great Rascal Flatts made it seem more like an off ramp.

But, it doesn't really matter who's singing the tune.

Just like the refrain from an old song, you finally reach your destination. When you pull in and park, you just have to wait. Let Aretha sing that last note, or listen to Jimi strike that final chord.

And when both your trip and the song finally end? That's when you realize that you're finally Home Sweet Home.

CHAPTER 23 | HERE COMES THE JUDGE

Do you ever wonder what the guy at the bank is thinking while he is counting your money? Or, if the folks at your church talk about what you were wearing after the service is over?

Well, worry no more, my friends. That's right, paranoia just ain't for ya.

In an age of free thought and even freer fashions, the opinions of others seem to carry less weight than a bellybutton ring. Sure, grandma may wear low-cut blouses, and the rumor is your uncle might be a pothead, but it's okay, kids. You be you.

That's because, nowadays, we take our first amendment rights to a whole, new level. No matter how outlandish your appearance, expression, or behavior, you aren't doing it to offend anyone, right?

You are just you trying to live life on your own terms, and you're pretty damn good at it. So, let your freak flag fly, baby.

In a perfect world, that's how we would deal with any conflict that threatens our individuality- just put our head down and bull forward.

By nature, people want to have the courage to strike out on their own, even though the pack tells us to stay close to the porch. You can become an outcast, based solely on your individuality.

Those who stand out, in any way, tend to be discussed at great length when they are not around. In some forms of science, this is called a social experiment in human interaction.

(Where I'm from, it's called "gossip".)

Be it the school board busybodies or the kids in the hall, somebody is always talking about somebody. Quite often, those stories aren't always true, and can really damage a person's psyche.

We've all experienced times where we felt like a complete and utter social outcast. Not because of our own decisions, but based on how others reacted to them.

Oddly, in a time when we are given so many choices when it comes to our lifestyle, we often find ourselves pigeonholed by the same handful of thoughts. Unfortunately, there's nothing you can do, except shake it off.

Like Bobby Brown said, it's your prerogative.

The only thing snickers are good for is making candy bars. All that heckling is just a tale told by an idiot... filled with the clowns in a jury.

That type of social judgement can be a terrible thing, especially if you let it bring its gavel down upon you.

The only person on this planet who knows everything that you've ever done wrong is you. From pulling the tag off the mattress and peeing in the shower, up to tax evasion and treason, you know every dirty stunt you've ever pulled.

Not them. Just you.

So, look in the mirror and open your eyes wide. Take inventory of what you are staring at, and then take into account all you know about yourself.

The opinion of the person you see is the only one that matters.

Because, my friends, when it comes to measuring your character, there is really only one ruler: Yourself.

CHAPTER 24 | THE BARBER OF DA' BILLS

Extra! Extra! ... Read all about it!

In the good old days, the sound of the your local newspaper hitting the driveway used to mean something. That brief daylight glimmer in your bathrobe, as you walk down your driveway, was a morning tradition.

Everyone would peel out their favorite pieces. Sports, comics, and local news are sectioned out among family members. That leaves behind only one thing: The chance to scissor up some savings in the advertising flyers. Get out the shears. It's time to cut costs by clipping coupons.

Whether it's 30% off or a once-in-a-lifetime offer, you can chop a lot off your weekly expenses by simply following along the dotted lines.

It's true. Coupons are a nice little bonus in your paper that reminds you how much your local businesses appreciate your patronage. For the customer, it's a chance keep more of their hard-earned money in their pocket.

And, extra cash is always good, no matter how you slice it.

But, keep your eyes peeled. Some of those offers will only be available for lunchtime only, or with proof of purchase. Others will be for adults 18 and older, and only while supplies last.

Every now and then, they're even valid in the United States AND Canada. That's awesome. It means you can save from Florida to Alaska, and all points in between. It's true. You can BOGO from Orlando to

Juneau.

Some coupons you have to mail in with a copy of your receipt in order to get a small refund back. I never understood that. It's like they don't mind giving you the money, but they want to see you put in a little extra effort for it.

Things have changed for newspapers and shoppers, however. With deals at the touch of a button, the old-fashioned way of shaving for savings is becoming pretty rare.

But for some of us, it's a reminder of simpler times.

For example, my grandmother used to snip along the edges of the ad section at the kitchen table. Then, she would hand me the shears to get whatever pictures and cartoons I wanted. What was left of Sunday's remains went flailing into the trash can.

Those times didn't just teach me about saving money. They educated me on what it was like to be an adult, waking up over coffee and bills. They made me happily await the newspaper every weekend. They're probably a big reason that I wanted for a paper someday.

Those days are gone, but I still find myself looking over the ad section. Maybe it's for nostalgia. Or, maybe it's just to save 30 cents a pound on steak.

Whatever your reasons, they're all justified. Clipping coupons is one of those quiet, simple things you can do to improve your life. Slicing out those Sunday savings is not only traditional, but economical as well.

After all, Everyone else is saving money. Why shouldn't you get your cut?

CHAPTER 25 | YOU *REALLY* SHOULDN'T HAVE

You say it's your birthday? It's my birthday, too.

Every year, June 30th marks the day of my birth, and as of now there have been almost 50 of them. That's a lot of years of highs, lows, and expired license stickers. It's a day to look back on life, for some.

I've never been a really big birthday person. I've actually only had two parties my entire life, and they were both surprises. I don't typically do a lot to celebrate, except cook or go out for a good meal. And to be honest, I have never been really comfortable receiving gifts.

Despite this, I find the gifting process fascinating in a macabre sort of way. On your most special of days, be prepared before you open your packages. You might get some things that not only tell you about yourself, but also what how your loved ones see you.

It starts out pretty basic. Your kids get you the usual birthday fare: socks, ties, or cologne. Sometimes, they make you a homemade meal that you happily eat, knowing that you'll be reaching for the Pepto Bismol later. Something about sugar cookies baked with chili powder just doesn't agree with your aging stomach.

Around the office, you may get a gift card or two. That's a passive way for a co-worker to say, "I don't really know you, or even like you. But I DO know everyone likes Applebee's!"

But hey... it's the thought that counts, right?

Older relatives get in on the action, too. Unfortunately, their gifts start to become a little dated over time. For example, that 10 dollars from Grandma was great when you were a kid, but inflation has deemed it almost useless in adulthood.

Even worse, the greeting cards that the cash comes in <u>used</u> to have cartoon characters on it. Now that you've aged, it's just a picture of an ominous, hazy sunset.

I've gotten a lot of bad gifts over the years. One time, my elderly aunt sewed me a pair of purple and gold mittens. She was in her 90's and couldn't see too well. So, I actually ended up with a three-toed sock and something that looked like a Crown Royal bag.

There are also those birthday reminders of how old you're actually getting. You know that you're starting to lose your mojo when you get a box of Odor Eaters or Super Poly-grip.

Or, when your girlfriend drops you a hint by giving you an Ab Buster. Apparently, she forgot about the one she bought you last year. It's still in the closet.

At some point, you might get dragged out to a meal, where the wait staff will sing you a bastardized version of the "Happy Birthday" song.

Because of trademark, they can't legally sing you the real thing. But if you're lucky, they might give you one of those dozen or so buttons they're wearing.

A couple of drinks never hurt either, right? Your buddies will eventually pry you away from all the quiet time to toast your life. They may even take you to a strip club for a birthday lap dance.

Nothing wrong with that, either. Just be sure to look, and don't touch. Otherwise, you may get a gift this year that you will be celebrating for all the years to come.

When the pointy hats come off and the wrapping's on the floor, you've added an extra digit to your identity. You have to rehearse what to say when people ask how old you are. You might even be tempted to lie about it a little.

Not me. I welcome June 30th like its my last.

I've had several birthdays since I was diagnosed with a terminal illness. I really never thought I was going to roll the odometer over once, let alone for almost a decade now. In that time, I've made some necessary improvements to my outlook on life.

So, I don't mind birthdays, I just don't think I need anymore presents. The best gifts of all were the mistakes I made in my past and the steps to correct them.

Because I've been handed regret, sorrow, and defeat, I'm able to celebrate everyday like its my birthday now. I'm also able to make positive changes in my life going forward, so that all my birthdays in the future are happy.

No matter how many of them I have left.

So, I'm not hoping for anything in particular this year. Not a set of pens for my office, a key chain, or a silly t-shirt. I don't need a Red Lobster appetizer or an ice cold beer. I've already been given enough.

Although, I've got to admit, I really *could* use a good set of salad forks.

CHAPTER 26 | CAME IN LIKE A CANNONBALL

You might want to put on your helmet and goggles for this one.

In the circus of life, we are all daredevils. Our exploits are like an event under Earth's big top. Our greatest moments and worst failures get played out in front of everyone, complete with all the pageantry and passion it deserves.

At least, that's what it feels like.

We often treat our lives like the guy in the circus who gets shot out of a cannon. His high-risk, low-reward approach to destiny is something we appreciate, because it's something we all do ourselves anyway.

When we take big steps, we are basically loading ourselves up to fly. No matter who lights our fuse, we're ready to go out with a boom.

Whether it's going to college or getting married, having a baby or having a cow, we are always on a ride that we have little control over.

As we shoot through the sky, we're not sure where we're going to land. But just like that courageous cannonballer, we believe the flight is worth the fate.

However, I'm sure that the daring circus performer with the cape gets nervous sometimes, too. Think about it: He's about to be a human projectile, so he's probably sweating bullets.

The thought of hurdling at a hundred miles an hour doesn't seem natural.

Yet, we do it in our own lives everyday, trying to navigate as best we can, while being blasted like a rocket. Unfortunately, many of our high-speed journeys end in crashes instead of congratulations. But, we never seem to get tired of hearing the boom, no matter how scary it can be.

I think that says something about our spirit as human beings. Even at zero gravity, we seem to always hold out hope for a safe landing.

That resiliency is something we not only admire in ourselves, but in others. The ability to face your daily fear is much like that of a circus ace.

Every time you open your door, you light the fuse and shoot out into the world. And you never know how it's going to end. It's either take a bow, or bow out in shame.

Through all of life's crash landings, people seem to always return to where they started... ready to be shot out of the cannon again.

And, as for me? I'm just the carnival barker

CHAPTER 27 | I AM LEGEND

They say you should never give yourself your own nickname. You're supposed to let other people do it for you.

After all, it's a little arrogant and presumptuous to assume everyone else is going to call you any moniker you just decide to tag yourself with.

One exception to the rule is if you actually *earn* that nickname.

Born in Louisville, KY, in 1942, Cassius Clay would eventually go on to become an Olympic gold medalist in boxing and the world heavyweight champion after becoming a pro.

Clay was different from most heavyweights of the time, because of his agility and stamina. Fight experts said that he was fast on his feet and a ring scientist. The media loved him, often referring to The Champ as handsome and charismatic.

Beyond that, he was considered the heir apparent to the great Joe Louis and hailed as the new standard of excellence for the sweet science.

That wasn't good enough for Clay, though. He anointed himself with the perfectly-tailored nickname, 'The Greatest.'

In the process, he also changed his legal name to Muhammad Ali, following his conversion to the Islamic faith in March 1964.

Ali was being advised by fiery civil rights leader Malcolm X, and in the years that followed, he became a spokesmen in the struggle for equality himself.

The World Champion's fame and outspokenness would push him to the forefront of the movement and make him a target of political enemies.

The firestorm that followed is well-documented, due to the fact that Ali's every move was watched closely. He may have been a polarizing figure, but everyone from the government, media, the fans, and boxing's governing body had a vested interest in his actions.

Socially, it was confusing for many people in this country who genuinely had no idea what Islam really even stood for. However, what little they did know sounded frightening to the folks in small towns and rural areas.

The public watched their new champion go through a muddled metamorphosis - His refusal for military service, being stripped of his title, a return to the ring and his eventual redemption in the court of public opinion.

With time and understanding, he went from being identified as a brash, traitorous villain to becoming a symbol of courage, dignity, and American popular culture.

But, no matter what they may have labelled him, he never changed his glorious nickname.

"I am the greatest. I said that even before I knew I was."

His fame grew as enormous as any athlete ever had. At one time more photographed than even the President, Ali morphed from a champion in the ring to an all-encompassing cultural phenomenon.

His face on talk shows drew ratings, even as his pomp and politics enraged some in mainstream America. Inevitably, the more famous he became and the more battles he fought, the more people started to listen to him as a man, and not just a brash boxer.

Also as pro sports' greatest trash-talker, he took advantage of the cameras and helped fuel one of the most successful eras of his sport.

So, the genius of Muhammad Ali's rhetoric served two purposes: It not only made dollars, it also made sense.

"He who is not courageous enough to take risks will accomplish nothing in life."

For many of his fellow citizens, he was a voice that shouted when so many others had been silenced. Ali's self-confidence and skill as a boxer was appreciated by men. His charm and humor made him attractive to women.

And his name gave him influence and power.

Muhammad Ali, the diplomat, certainly changed the world based on the appreciation and understanding he garnered in his later years. Ali, the brand, continues to make millions of dollars to this day. And needless to say, the mark he left on boxing will last forever.

That mark includes the nickname "The Greatest". While it can be argued whether or not he was the best fighter of all time, there's no denying he was the most famous. Without his excellence, there may not be the huge purses and pay-per-views that followed.

Ali also blazed a trail for athletes of any sport and any color to engage in political and social activism.

"Service to others is the rent you pay for your room here on earth."

For many people, the sporting world is something they don't pay attention to and don't even think about much. They can't tell you who the starting pitcher is that night, or even when the game starts. As famous as some athletes seem to be, the average person can't normally pick them out of a crowd.

A select few others achieve a fame and iconic status where they transcend their sports.

Everybody from your grandma to your girlfriend knows who they are. And, they are simply called by one name. Jordan, Pele, Gretzky...

Ali.

Or, "The Greatest", as he often liked to be called.

CHAPTER 28 | THE FICKLE FOUR SEASONS

Sometimes, figuring out the weather is like being caught up in a bad romance.

Recently, we've seen a mixture in our climate that can only be described as radical. In between our rampant summers and moody winters, it forces you to guess every day whether to choose between a sweater or some shades.

The bitch fits displayed by our current weather patterns resemble that of a fickle girlfriend, where both hot and cold flow at the flip of a switch. When she gets moody, you can expect a lot of rain and thunder. But, if everything's alright, there are some really sweet and sunny days.

The only difference is that a relationship takes months - sometimes years - to really cultivate. Meanwhile, the wind blows at a much brisker pace than that.

The other day started out just like a first date. It was surprisingly warm out, and a gentle breeze let me know that the trip to the mailbox required a light jacket or at least a sweatshirt. Much like a first date, it was pleasant and not too overwhelming.

I stepped out again around noon, to find that it was downright hot!

Things had really moved along. I was falling in love with this weather, completely head over heels with visions of shorts and tank tops. Surely, I couldn't be thinking of breaking out the grill this early?

My heart began to flutter. It was like a total June swoon, except in February. I mean, I wasn't ready to marry this weather yet, but I certainly had no problem living with it.

I started to feel comfortable. I kicked my feet up, satisfied with my environment. Her sweet and warm embrace felt so nurturing.

Then, without warning, she changed on me. I guess I wasn't paying attention, because when I looked out my window a few hours later, I saw some dark clouds. A blustery wind was getting awfully pushy out there.

As I started out the door to to take out some trash, I felt a blast of arctic air. It was like *literally* getting the cold shoulder. I hurried back in to grab a jacket, suddenly thinking that this relationship was headed in the wrong direction.

I'm not sure what I did, but at some point the weather became angry with me. Despite my hopes for sunshine, by nightfall, it was ball-shaking cold.

The warm feeling of only a few hours earlier was gone. With one last, frigid kiss, the glorious hope of the morning hours had disappeared. I had loved, and I had lost. Now, I felt totally frozen out.

I went from delighted to disappointed with the climate in the span of just one day. It was the second-shortest relationship I have ever been in.

So, beware before you invest your emotions in our fickle, Midwest weather. You might have your heart broken like a storm window in a tornado.

CHAPTER 29 | I SCREAM, YOU SCREAM

There's nothing like a double scoop of goodness, complete with the sprinkles.

Have you ever heard anyone say that they *hate* ice cream? Seriously, it may be the one comfort food that we can all agree on. Unless you're lactose intolerant, there's no reason to not enjoy a spoonful of spun cold.

Like all great inventions, ice cream can come in many forms. This multi-purpose treat can come as a sundae or a cone. It can be frozen or soft serve. No matter what your desires, ice cream can fill them, even if you want to shake it up a bit. The options are limitless.

You've got everything from Raspberry Ripple to Blue Moon, or Pistachio to Spumoni. Thanks to a couple of guys named Baskin and Robbins, you can just pick your pleasure.

Believe it or not, ice cream can also be considered a health food. Not only being a great source of calcium, a bag of fudge bars can also serve as a compress during a really bad headache.

And for reasons I have never understood, medical science has concluded that ice cream also (somehow) cures tonsillitis. So, basically it's the most delicious elixir you can ever take, you know?

In any political year, the hard-edged Republican Party loves Rocky Road. Democrats (always trying to impossibly please everyone) go with butter pecan. The official flavor of the Libertarian Party is strawberry, mainly because they both always seem to be everyone's last choice.

Neapolitan includes all the major flavors, which may be a bit socialist, but delicious, nonetheless.

I have to be honest: Sherbet has always been a mystery to me. It looks like ice cream and has similar properties but it's different. It's kind of like a stunt double. It fills the role when the real thing isn't available.

And, don't even get me started on Gelato.

There's never a bad time for ice cream, so please don't feel guilty. A few more Pilates is a good enough reason for a couple extra scoops of cookies 'n' creme.

Maybe a girl just broke up with her boyfriend, or a coach is taking his little league bunch out for a treat after the game. It doesn't matter the reason, just grab a half-quart of happiness and just chill.

Load up a bowl full of chocolate, vanilla, and strawberry together. Drown it in syrup and cover it in whipped cream. Feel free to throw a cherry on top. If you need more toppings, just go nuts!

Armed with nothing but a spoon and an aggressive palate, it's time to tear into a mountain of calories.

But, one word to the wise: Just don't dive in too fast.
You might end up with a headache.

CHAPTER 30 | TECHNICALLY SPEAKING

How fast is the world moving? Let me tell you, neighbor…

The other day, I found myself watching the TV on mute while working on my laptop. I had music in one ear and my phone's headset in the other.

After the call, I had to shut everything off, and ask myself: Wait a minute. Did I just order a pizza from Pink Floyd? It was so confusing.

Welcome to the wonderful world of information overload. It seems we can't get enough of our inflation of communication.

Our desire to know, say, and hear more drives today's technology like a tank through glass. For example, people who could afford them used to carry cellphones for emergency situations. Now, they are used to randomly transmit to the world what we're eating for lunch.

It's no longer a luxury; we *need* it. We just have to touch the world in some way, and why not do it from long distance?

High-speed internet service fuels this fire. The quicker and the quieter the data can be dispersed, the better.

Today's technology moves at an almost alarming pace, and no longer makes even a crackle when it does. (Can you believe it's only been a little over ten years since dial-up went the way of the Death Star?)

Now, the scan of a bar code or the click of a mouse gives you instant access to everything: food, shopping, and tickets to next month's Monster

Truck Show.

You can do just about everything pretty rapidly and without the inconvenience of dealing with those pesky things called humans. I mean, you have a firewall for a reason.

In the present day, the options are endless. A simple call is often replaced by a Facebook message. You can voice record your grocery list, or fire off a tweet to Sarah Jessica Parker.

Lord knows, I have. (The grocery thing, I mean.)

Which brings us to another rage of communication: texting. Cellphones have now become tiny typewriters where we send out digital smoke signals - in some sort of language that aliens invented. Kids today would laugh hysterically at the mere thought of having a real and meaningful conversation. Or, they would at least type 'LOL'.

It's not just people either. Even your computer seems to be giving us the silent treatment. Sadly, nobody even bothers to tell you that "you've got mail", anymore.

So, basically, it's like a lot of talking without really talking. For example, we live in the era of the 'angry text message'.

Really? Are we that passive-aggressive? We're so mad that we take the damn time to type out how much? (And yes, I'm guilty of this myself.)

I guess it's a foregone conclusion that this trend won't change. Fireside chats have been replaced by online chats. People now Skype dinner dates. And, somewhere along the way, our dialogue turned digital.

It's quick, it's casual, and it's convenient. I'm just not sure it's really 'communicating', is it?

CHAPTER 31 | MAN VS. MOUSE

Any noise that you hear as you are about to fall asleep is annoying. When you realize that noise is coming from inside your house from an unwelcome visitor, it's time to panic.

It's not an intruder of the ordinary sort. This interloper is small, furry, and fast. He enjoys chewing through everything in your house, and though I'm not sure, may have done some time in prison. Probably, Mexico.

He is my nemesis in life: the mouse.

I may hate mice more than snakes or any other vermin on Earth. Filthy, destructive, and disease-ridden, they are not welcome in my home. Even their cold, calculating little eyes remind me of those characters in the "Spy vs. Spy" section of Mad Magazine.

Needless to say, I can't sleep when I hear the sickening scratches of a mouse that has decided to hitch a ride in my boxcar.

Upon rising, I quickly assessed where my target was: the bathroom. I quickly searched for a broom, only to realize I needed to start keeping better shopping lists. Putting a broom on one of those lists would be a nice start.

Back to the mouse. I entered the bathroom holding a shoe, and he spotted me immediately. I could tell he was going to make break for it, so I swung a mighty Adidas in his direction.

Then, he jumped. But not forward, in the usual way.

In mid-stride, he shot straight up in the air, like Super Mario, and landed safely on his little feet. Even the French judges would have scored it a ten.

Feeling desperate and scared, I grabbed a bottle of bleach and fired it, screaming like Rambo. He was blinded, just like his three cousins had been years before. Suddenly stunned, he re-grouped for a bit. The burning in his eyes only seemed to fuel his desire to destroy my house and my life.

Finally, the fumes were too much, and he surrendered. I gave my disgusting yet worthy adversary an honorable burial in the trash can.

I settled back into bed, comfortably pleased with a job well done. The pace of my heart slowed down, and I had rid myself of a terrifying foe. It was finally time to drift back to sleep peacefully...

Wait a minute. What was that noise?
That's it. I'm sleeping with the lights on.

CHAPTER 32 | BREAKING UP IS HARD TO DO

Some guys have all the luck. Some guys have dumb luck. Then, with a select few other men, there's no luck at all. They're just dumb, and they're easy to spot, too.

He's that dude chasing after his girlfriend in the mall, begging for a second chance. She isn't having it, either. There's usually some hand waving and maybe a curse word or two. He struggles to keep pace as he pulls up his Dockers and grasps a mocha latte. What did this poor idiot do?

The answer is nothing. And everything, depending on who you ask.

See... he got up to get her a soda, but forgot to tell them to add crushed ice instead of cubes. So, she's mad. After all, she told him that's what she wanted. Six years ago. She remembers it clearly, because it was on a Tuesday back in June.

Now, she's staring at this clueless fool, seething with anger inside. Look at him, with that stupid grin on his face like he's proud of himself. He returns, smiling politely. She looks at the drink, smirks, and throws it on him.

They end their magical three-week relationship right there. De-friended on Facebook, even!

Welcome to Breaking Up 101. Take your seats, but only after you've been searched for weapons. And yes, frying pans are considered weapons, kids.

The cosmic forces that bring people together and tear them apart work like a pendulum. On one side is the smooth sway of the courting process, the other is like the swinging blade of an ax murderer. It's quite a dramatic process, all captured in photographs. Photographs that will later be torn in half, by the way.

So, how did they get there? Well, let's face the facts: For the most part, people are annoying creatures by our nature. More than one of us together too long is like chewing on tin foil. Every fault, habit, and mannerisms is there to be judged by another individual.

They watch incredulously as you lick the salt off your fries. You can't believe they bought that scarf. It becomes a game of who can pick the most nit.

We don't say anything, until the stress gets to be too much. This typically occurs sometime in traffic. Or when you forgot to pay the bills.

Or when your drunk friends puke on the floor again. (Thanks, Mikey.)

At this point, everything you have ever done remotely wrong comes to the surface. You strike back firing shots at them in rapid succession.

Before long the past reputation of someone's mother is brought into the fray. That's when its gone too far. Cooler heads just have to prevail here, right?

So, they settle down. Everything's okay and it can all be worked out. With red faces drenched in sweat and tears, they hug and promise to never fight again.

She suggests lunch. He agrees, and softly tells his baby that they can eat anywhere she wants. As they sit together, they stare into each other's eyes.

That's when she looks at him, bats her thick eyelashes and sweetly asks,"Can you go get me another soda, sweetie?"

CHAPTER 33 | RAIDERS OF THE LOST BARK

Termites are the worst kind of pest. Next to people, that is.

I say this only because I actually saw a termite the other day. I haven't seen one in years, besides the depictions you see in Bugs Bunny cartoons that can shear a tree into a toothpick within seconds. No. I'm talking about an actual, real life termite.

It led me to wonder: How much wood does a termite terminate? And what motivates these guys to destroy homes and lives with their appetite for oak?

The common termite is scientifically classified in the order Isoptera, but these guys actually have no class at all. Like strangers with the munchies, they bust into your crib, breaking down your base with their bite. They chip away, leaving only loose wall outlets behind at the murder scene.

And, they don't apologize for it, either. Asking a termite to say he's sorry will just leave you pining away.

When you think about it, people are similar in that way. Like those block-headed bugs, there are just some folks who are uninvited guests in your home or your life. And, certain interlopers can cause more serious damage than others.

The most destructive people in your life will chew you up from the inside out if you let them, just like a termite. The only question is, will you let them sell you some kind of wooden nickel?

Everyone is vulnerable at times. Whenever we forget to fumigate our homes and our lives, that's when the predators will attempt to take advantage of the situation.

Often, your fellow exterminators will notice that you have a particularly pesky problem before you even realize it. The ones closest to you usually help you keep your stakes in the ground.

Unfortunately, termites have their own army, too. They mobilize as a unit, relying on strength in numbers to make up for their lack of intelligence and relative obscurity. People do this a lot, too.

They say to keep friends close and enemies closer. That certainly doesn't hit the nail on the head when it comes to these pests. As if drunk on sap, termites recklessly take what they want. Keeping them close would be like inviting a fat guy with the munchies to Red Lobster. My advice: stay at least a yardstick away.

People tend to act in the same selfish, take-it-all ways. Oftentimes, we look past the common good of our environment in exchange for gluttony.

It's seemingly never enough with some folks, as they don't mind breaking down the structure of your life and reducing it to sawdust.

And just like people, termites will combine forces for their common goal. They will gather together, taking great pleasure in taking away something you hold dear. They will disrupt your life, like a friend who looms in the shadows, only to reveal himself later as a foe.

It's a scary thought, the idea that someone or something can chew holes through the walls we use to protect ourselves. Unfortunately, we forget that we not only have to guard "Home Sweet Home", but our "Fortress of Feelings" as well.

After all, there's some things in life even insurance can't replace. Some things belong to only you, and shouldn't be on any pest's menu.

So, just like termites, you should watch who you let in.

They might just eat you out of house and soul.

CHAPTER 34 | REUNITED, AND IT FEELS...

When you live in the Midwest, the Autumn season always seems to ring in some good old traditions. Brown leaves and football games mean that the warm weather's coming to an end, and we've only got so much luxurious leisure time left.

You've got to take advantage of it, right?
I mean, there is only so much precious daylight that we're no longer going to save, so what should we do?

The traditional family reunion, of course.

I use the term 'traditional' in a very loose way. In these parts, a family gathering can mean everything from outlaws to in-laws. There's always a mystery cousin who shows up and never speaks, but eats three plates of food. I think his name's Paul. And now that I think of it, he isn't a cousin. That's just Frank's nephew from his third marriage.

Yes, in a scene something out of the 'Grapes of Wrath', the entire family Joad descends upon someone's house. Your house. Every year. That's what you get for being the relative with the good outhouse.

It could be worse. The year we had to hold our annual get-together at a rest area was a disaster. To be fair, however, it was also where Mary Lou met that trucker. (He's your Uncle Jake now.)

No doubt about it, the fall family reunion puts the 'fun' back in the word dysfunctional.

Between all the mystery meat and green Jell-O with things floating in it, there is plenty of (stuff) to eat. Bellies are filled, and a calm falls over the crowd. Pictures of allegedly *adorable* children are displayed. A warm buzz dances in the air. Over in the corner, a quiet six year old chews on a Styrofoam cup.

At this point, it's kind of pleasant. You almost don't mind having to hear the detailed story of how you can tell the twins apart.

Suddenly, chaos ensues. Word leaks out that someone's brother is dating a girl that an adopted cousin once had a couple of drinks with six years ago.

Needless to say, blood is no longer thicker than water, and it's all-out warfare! A couple head butts, some girls slap fighting and pulling hair, leading to a broken lamp or coffee table.

Finally, everyone is separated and bygones become bygones. After all, everyone is still family, right?

When all the dust has cleared, and the bodies have been counted, it's coat check time. The only thing left for weary travelers now is to return from whence they came.

Packing some form of chicken inside of orange Tupperware, they begin to say their goodbyes. They start to wrap up those goodbyes approximately three hours later.

The last hug and handshake, that final goodbye and good riddance. All of it summed up with one final refrain.

It's a statement about your wobbly, crazy crew that just keeps on going, no matter what happens at the family reunion. So take care, and as always...

See you next year.

CHAPTER 35 | KICKBALL

I would like to share some information I have acquired after nearly 48 years of everyday research: *Not everything* that didn't go my way when I was a kid is a traumatic experience. It may sound very elementary, but for many, this line of thinking still remains a mystery.

Some parts of our past - particularly from our childhood and adolescence - seem to just haunt us for eternity, don't they? They stick to us like some sort of depressing glue. And it must be some really good glue, because it holds on forever.

And no matter what we try to do to scrub it from our memories? It still always leaves a greasy stain behind.

It's all the BS stuff that people (for whatever reason) carry around, that everyone but you has already forgotten about.

Why? Do we really think that people we haven't seen in years sit around and ponder the most embarrassing moments in our lives?

Or, are we just so paranoid and self-absorbed that feel like EVERYONE must remember that moment about us! How embarrassing!

People have legitimate reasons for aversions to their past if it was truly awful. In that situation, there has to be cause for concern, and you can only hope that they don't harm themselves or turn to addiction when they can't find any answers.

But the majority of our 'baggage' - at least for the average person - is ours, and ours, alone. We spend our whole lives packing it until it gets harder and harder to carry around. Eventually, it just frustrates you, but you have to keep lugging it along, wherever you go.

I'll give you an example.
When I was a kid, we all lined up to choose sides for a rousing recess full of kickball. And at my school? It got pretty intense, man. It was time to kill or be killed. Winner-take-all.

At least, until the bell rang.

Unfortunately, I contracted Scarlet Fever when I was only six years old, and for quite a while after, I was a pretty small and sickly kid. In fact, I really didn't start growing until about the eighth grade, but ended up being 6'2" and around 200 pounds in the end.

But prior to that, I basically had the physique of the average person's X-Ray, and didn't look like much of a kickball player.

Therefore, I would often get picked last, or sometimes not at all. So, I would watch while the other kids played, and they (of course) thought it was hilarious. Even the girls were making fun of me.

I hated that. But I got over it, and at the end of the day, I realized my friends were just giving me a hard time. They weren't trying to 'scar me for life'.

And besides, the joke's on them anyway. No matter how much any of them ran around out there, not ONE ever became a professional kickball player.

So it turns out, it was all just a waste of time.
Just like worrying about it was a waste of time.

Sometimes I think that as much as we think the world is laughing at us, it's really just ourselves trying to justify our own shortcomings. We don't like being made to feel inferior.

Some people lash out, but most just hold it in and let it bother them. Forever. And like a form of cancer, it eats them up inside.

We also tend to do this with the most irrelevant of events and people, as well. Most of the folks that we associate with those kinds of memories are usually so far removed from our lives that, for all we know, they may not even be alive anymore.

But it wouldn't matter, because some moment they held over you years ago, if only briefly, still bothers you like you've got a horde of bees in your bonnet.

You shouldn't worry about it. It didn't define you then, and it certainly doesn't say anything about who you are TODAY.

So please, if you ever find yourself on a psychiatrist's couch, and he asks you what's wrong?

Please don't start off by saying: "Well, it all started that time I didn't get picked for kickball..."

CHAPTER 36 | THE CREAM OF THE CROP

When bringing up the greatest snack foods of all time, it's easy to go to the usual, timeless favorites. Potato chips or hard candy immediately come to mind. However, I contend that there is an even nuttier contender out there for this made-up award.

Peanut butter may be a gift from the gods. It's the perfect snack food, and I am more than happy to explain why. So, I will be the host with the toast, as we take a look at this supermarket sensation.

Way back before there was sunlight, some really important dude named Carver invented peanut butter. Or, perfected it. I'm not sure which, really. Maybe someone knows all about the subject and they're just keeping a lid on it.

All I know is, peanut butter is like the utility man of snack foods. Bread, celery, crackers, and even your finger can instantly transport this magical spread - from jar, to mouth, to stomach.

During my first marriage, I even did a little social experiment involving the peanut butter in our cabinet. I found that if I ate all of it out of the jar with a spoon, that I had to sleep on the couch.

I documented all my notes on the subject and did further testing later. All with the same results.

As far as the nutritional value, it contains all kinds of good stuff, like thiamine, protein and vitamin E. It also helps people who are sick or underweight add healthy mass to their frame. So, it sticks to your ribs almost as much as it sticks to the roof your mouth.

This dark, tan goo is so delicious that mice apparently jump onto traps for it, trying to make a scoop-and-run. That never seems to work out well for the ravenous rodent, and with a mouthful of muck, they can't even scream for help.

Peanut butter also makes regular appearances in all kinds of sticky stuff like cookies, cakes, and candy bars. Yet, it can allegedly still somehow remove gum that's stuck in your hair. That's not only versatile; it's simply amazing.

Much like with American politics, you only have two choices - creamy or chunky. You can put me down in the category of a creamy fan. Some might say we're 'too soft', but I've found the folks who prefer the crunchy stuff to be too abrasive. I guess might say that makes me a jackass.

Also, the kind with all the crunchy bits tear the bread that it's smeared across. The only cure for that is more peanut butter, so it's a delicious cycle.

Of course, you can't invoke the name of peanut butter, without also mentioning it's goofy stepbrother, jelly. Unlike reliable, old peanut butter, jelly will often change it's style from red, to purple, to orange. It has several different personalities.

You would think this pair of polar opposites wouldn't mesh well, but they actually do. In fact, when the two spreadable snacks get together, it's like when the Eagles have a reunion concert. Well, maybe not quite *that* big. PB & J has always been more of a 'jam' band.

Peanut butter is a very noble food, as well. If it ever got arrested, I'm quite certain that it would cooperate with the police. It's always ready to spread 'em.

Now that you've gotten the Skippy on this jar full o' goodness, stand up and toastify. Peanut butter is the perfect paste for the palate, ruling the snack food universe with a knife that could cut... (well, you know.)

What I'm saying is, it's not just for bread anymore. Peanut butter is a must for any healthy home, and it's greatness cannot be denied. It's the snack food that choosy moms choose. And why?

Because peanut butter makes everything better.

CHAPTER 37 | SYMBOL-MINDED THINKING

Sometimes an eagle is just an eagle.

He's fine with that; he couldn't be happier. As a matter of fact, an eagle never asked to be inscribed on coins or painted on monuments. But, unbeknownst to him, he's the spokesperson for the world's most powerful nation.

He wasn't trying to be a hero, he was just out hunting for dinner.

But, for some reason, we find meaning in that powerful bird and what he stands for. Just like many things in our life, that winged warrior is a symbol. And you know what symbols do? They stand for something, damn it.

You know what I'm talking about: images, from classic logos all the way to graffiti on bridges. They're the markings that let you know the who's-who, and the what's-what. Symbols represent all sorts of people, places, and things.

They're everywhere, too. Anything of substance has its own personalized artwork to distinguish itself. We know the fish symbol for Jesus almost as much as we know what the New York Yankees logo looks like.

They make a statement. Wearing a Nike swoosh lets everybody know that hit the gym regularly. Donning a pink ribbon shows them that you hate breast cancer, right?

That's right. Signs, signs, everywhere there's signs, baby.

Some symbols are even used to mark style and beauty. As every pageant winner will tell you: If you like it, you better put a sash on it.

But, you have to pick your insignia properly. For example, a swastika probably isn't the best design for your welcome mat. It doesn't really seem very warm and cuddly.

And, you probably shouldn't wear that pot leaf t-shirt to a job interview, unless you're applying to be a taste tester for Frito Lay.

You don't want to over-symbol-fy things, either. That's when it can get ugly. Before you know it, that royal emblem matters more itself than what it's actually supposed to stand for.

Even our nation's flag faces this same paradox: Is it a symbol of national pride and unity, or just a really colorful use of propaganda? Depending on how you view things, it could be either. Or, even worse- both.

I'm not an anarchist. I'm certainly not suggesting that we desecrate graves or burn flags. If someone has pride in their nation and chooses to use Old

Glory as a way to let the world know, more power to them. I just wonder if they realize where all that emotion really comes from.

That's because, often times, we worry more about standing up for that symbol than we do standing up for our fellow man.

Recently, a huge debate over the confederate flag ended with it being taken down from government buildings in the south. It was hailed by many as a victory.

While I was fully in favor of the move, it left me with just a couple of questions. In the grand scheme of things, did it strike out what happened in the past? No. Did it fix the economic disadvantages that the time period forced upon the current generation? No.

All it did was make everybody feel a lot better about it. That's all, and nothing more. And that's unfortunate, because it seems like our priorities should lie somewhere greater than that.

And that's what symbols are, a style-over-substance play on our emotions. Good flag, bad flag… It doesn't matter. It's not really about the symbol itself, but more about the people behind it. Sadly, we fall for it all anyway.

Now, look back at our friend, the eagle, and ask yourself a couple of questions:

Does our society relate to him because he is strong and powerful? Or, is it because we know - deep down - that we're both an endangered species?

CHAPTER 38 | CLASS, TAKE YOUR SEATS

They say you never forget your very first really big experiences in life. Perhaps it's your first love, or the day you could finally drive legally, but those watershed moments always seem to have a special place in your heart.

We grow fonder and fonder of these moments as we get older. Maybe it's part of the circle of life. Or something philosophical like that.

To this day, I can still remember my first day of school. Walking up to that little brick building with my Mom, it was like a whole new world.

Even now - over 40 years later - I really don't recall a whole lot about my childhood, but I can always take myself back to that moment in an instant.

The sight, sounds, and smell of the place were totally foreign to me. Everything seemed like it was really big and moving so fast. And all I kept thinking in my little mind was: 'Yeah, um, there's no way I'm staying at this place. I'll give it a day or two. Maybe a week, tops'.

Describing the small, Midwestern town I grew up in as undersized would be a huge understatement. It had a population of around 1,000 people, and it was located in deep, southern Illinois. In the delta area normally referred to as 'Little Egypt', there are a lot of these same specks on the map.

My circle of friends, too, was rather small. As in non-existent. I grew up out in the country. And when I wasn't with my Mom, I was watched by my two grandmothers.

I didn't play outside much and didn't really know a lot of kids outside of my own family. So, this was really my initial encounter with social anxiety.

Our school (like everything else) was also tiny. Grades K-12 all went through one, long, connected building. You would essentially start on one side as a little kid, and graduate on the other as a young adult.

So, it was kind of like an assembly line for an education. The vast majority of my classmates and I went all the way through those 13 years together. We graduated in the Spring of 1993.

But it was the Fall of 1980 when we took our first steps toward higher learning. And it was then that I met someone who would shape my life forever - Mrs. Bradley, my kindergarten teacher.

She was young, intelligent, and kind. And although I was certain that she didn't have kids of her own yet, she had an amazing maternal instinct.

I'm not sure if that came to her naturally, or from being so idyllic. Mrs. Bradley just always had a way to make you feel better about yourself, with just a smile or a hug.

And she was beautiful. Elegant and pristine, she looked so impressive that you just knew that whatever she was saying was important. As a little guy, I wasn't sure exactly how smart she was, I just knew that I wanted to be as smart as her *someday*.

As mentioned previously, I was incredibly wary of school and all the people there. I was - for lack of a better term - scared out of my wits. Everything in my little world was changing, and life was rapidly expanding. And now? I was being taken out of my comfort zone and forced to spend my day around a bunch of strangers.

But Mrs. Bradley helped ease all of my fears. She was very caring and compassionate. For a kid who had basically been babied for most of their childhood, she was like my 'School Mom' until I could really get used to being there.

She made me feel brave enough to face it all. (And yes, I was one of those children who would sometimes cry, because they wanted to go home.)

She made me actually *like* school. And that made me want to learn more. So I guess as a teacher? Mrs. Bradley really knew what she was doing, eh?

More than anything, she gave me a belief that there are people out there who care. Not just in teaching, but in all professions. Some people just have the heart and the fortitude to make an impact. And often, it's a bigger positive than they may even realize.

I ran into Mrs. Bradley a few years ago, and she was the same as ever. Still vibrant, fun, and lovely, she's retired now and enjoying life. And that makes me happy. To know that out of all the stories she read to us in class, her life and career turned out to have a happy ending, too.

I learned a lot of things from Mrs. Bradley, like math, spelling, and reading. But I also learned from her that we can all make a difference if we just care enough to pour our hearts into what we do.

Oh yeah?

She also taught me that right after lunch is a great time to take a nap.

CHAPTER 39 | CANDLELIGHT

When the countdown to turning 40 started, a milestone in life, I could hardly wait. No, really… most people hate that day, but not me. I was downright excited about approaching middle age, as crazy as that may sound to some folks.

You see, 40 wasn't supposed to happen the way that it did. Not for me. Not in this life.

It's not because I wouldn't be getting the gifts I wanted, or because some vacation plans unexpectedly fell through. Trivial little things like that weren't on my mind anymore.

That's because turning 40 wasn't really supposed to happen at all.

On October 20th, 2014, I checked into my local hospital with a severe case of jaundice - a yellowing of the skin caused by liver problems. After 20 years of a serious addiction that I tried to pass off as no big deal, the evidence was now written all over my face.

I was a drunk. And, drinking was making me sick.
Sicker than I had already been thinking that I might be.

Upon taking blood, physicians advised me that a normal bilirubin count for a healthy liver should register somewhere between 0.5 and 1.25.

The potential lethal level is 17.5 and above. Mine was **36.3**.

It was so astoundingly high that even the staff on hand couldn't believe I was conscious and speaking to them as if nothing was wrong. By most medical standards, I should have probably been in a coma.

I was dying, and the decision to transfer me to one hospital, then another, was made swiftly. Doctors told me little, but I knew something bad was happening. I could feel it in my churning guts and by the look of shock and panic looks on the faces of the random medical staff.

When I finally arrived, I received the finest care. Or at least that's what everyone tells me. Apparently, my first few days there were spent in a coma that was half-medication, half-detoxification.

Doctors advised my father they estimated I had about two weeks to live and asked him if he knew my final wishes. Meanwhile in my hospital bed, my body and mind were going into shock. From what I was told later, I had to be physically restrained at various times.

Also in that same span, I became irrational with my nurses and defecated in my own bed, just so they would have to clean it up. At least, I guess that's why. I don't really remember any of it.

I do remember how I got there, though.

I discovered the joys of alcohol around the ripe, old age of 19, although I was admittedly a small-town kid who spent a good chunk of his adolescence around bars and pubs.

My grandfather used to take us to the neighborhood watering hole when he would 'babysit' us. So it was no big deal when I got to college and started hanging out with an older crowd. I had been there before. I could handle it.

In fact? By the time I was 18, I already had more experience drinking than a lot of people in their 20's did. So I just fell in with the group and went wherever the good times took me.

The twenty years that followed were almost like a train wreck of heartbreak and emotion, brought on by my own bottle-toting hand. Every door that opened almost closed immediately.

I became a totally different guy as my mood and my mojo both changed. I spent 16 years being a nuisance to a wife who finally got tired of it and left me, but kept our two little girls as a souvenir.

The desperate need and desire to get drunk may have been the scariest part of my addiction. It was like a job. I would get up and plan my day around my drinking schedule, not the other way around.

Sometimes it was difficult to manage on a tight budget. I remember reaching under my car seats, scraping my knuckles on the jagged metal underneath them, trying to retrieve loose change to buy a cold one. Gathering up a few quarters and nickels was a good way to quench your thirst.

But, I had a rule. I would never pay for my booze with pennies. No, sir. Only a drunk would do that, right?

I did anything I could to maintain that fuzzy feeling. I neglected my work, ignored my wife and kids, and burned bridges with friends and family. When I was inevitably unemployed, I sometimes worked odd jobs for cases of beer. I would lean on old buddies to buy me just one more round.

I borrowed money from my parents and would go visit friends just because I knew they had a cold one waiting for me in their 'fridge.

For god's sake, I even pawned my wife's wedding ring for it.

Then there's the time my youngest daughter watched her father having an alcohol-induced seizure. Lying there, unable to speak, I thought that's how she was going to end up remembering me: as a helpless and floundering victim of my own insanity.

She was only four years old at the time and was rightfully scared and confused. And had I died right then and there? She would have been forced to spend the rest of her life trying to make sense of it all.

I curled up in that hospital bed and thought that I had finally gotten what I deserved. All those years of giving the best part of me away to booze and only showing my dark side to others had come to cash its check. I deserved to go right then and there, a miserable memory of human failure.

The story does have a happy conclusion, however. You see, I actually end up living in the end.

I made a decision late in the night on the seventh floor of that hospital. As I lay in bed, scared of the dark - a grown man, frightened by something that had not bothered him since he was a small child.

Cold rooms and dimmed lights were grim reminders of what was going on around me. I listened to other patients let out growls of anguish. They were noises like I had never heard before and I could only think one thing. That must be the sound you make when your life is slowly leaving your body.

On this particular night, I heard one of those sounds finally come out of me. I got scared and cried, quietly, to myself. It couldn't be this dark anymore. No matter how much shade headed in my direction, I had to be like a flashlight.

And, now, there was no playing around and no other choice. I would have to shine brighter than I ever had before, against all odds and with little room for error.

That's when I lifted my head, maybe in desperation or possibly in a stubborn belief that it wasn't quite over just yet. I began searching for the light, no matter how flickering it may have been. After all, alcohol had sucked the life out of me like a vampire, and we all know what kills vampires, right?

It's a scary thing, knowing that every fiber of your being has to go into saving just one person… yourself.

But these days, it's more than that. I started listening to my physicians, often going beyond what they asked me to do, and I even came up with little rituals and tricks to take my mind off drinking.

It became a fight for me, and the anger I had for the world was soon redirected and aimed at those damn brown bottles. They couldn't do this to me anymore. I wouldn't let them hurt me again.

Amidst all this, I found clarity and happiness that is still a little foreign to me. Outside of never stepping into a bar and avoiding some friends who are (quite frankly) bad influences, I have found other health improvements that I never thought I would enjoy.

I eat right and generally try to live a healthy, active life. I'm happy to report that my doctors have seen substantial progress and feel I am making good strides.

And, I feel great. I made contact again with my daughters, and my oldest lives with me now. I have a hope that the youngest one will eventually decide she wants to come here, too. Then, we can finally be a family again.

I can't do all the things I used to do before, but that's okay. I make adjustments. My life is different now, but at least I have one. Out of all the people who were on that hospital floor with me, I'm one of only a handful who lived, and one of even fewer that go on to have a basically normal life.

I got lucky and got a break that probably a million other people deserved more than I did. So, I decided that I wasn't going to waste it. Everything I taste now has to be savored, every moment remembered, and every single birthday celebrated.

Not just for me, but for the people who didn't get the same, wonderful gift that I was lucky enough to be granted. To see my birthday candles lit up every year, and somehow miraculously still be here to blow them out.

When all the good time fireworks and party explosions finally flame out, it leaves behind a dense, gray spot in this world. And at times, that's where you lie, awaiting either death or redemption.

There are a lot of nights spent staring at a ceiling, yours or a stranger's, and wondering how you ended up renting your own, personal basement in hell.

That's when it's time to come up with an escape plan.

That journey begins with feeling your way through what seems like an eternity of shadows. It starts out slow, but after a while, it's like riding a bike. You may get lost or even go in circles sometimes, but somehow you'll know where you're headed.

And when you get there, *don't worry…* I'll leave the light on for you.

FINAL CHAPTER | THE BUS RIDE

At first glance, it seemed like some kind of mythical forest, with the sweet smell of flowers and fruit in the air. There was a field of perfect, emerald grass, and it looked so soft that I wanted to walk on it, and the it sent a rush of euphoria all the way from my feet up to my soul.

"Go on, now," the driver said. Then, he drove off.

I still wasn't sure where I was, so I sat down right there and had a picnic. There were marijuana plants there. Naturally, I smoked a little bit to calm my nerves.

What I didn't know, was where all that stuff came from. I just know that I looked down and it was there. As a matter of fact? I still wasn't sure where I was, but I really didn't care. Because it seemed like such a happy place. And everything I thought about was suddenly at my disposal and mine for the taking.

I ate the finest steak I'd ever tasted in my life, and I washed it down with red wine so sweet that it felt like it was dancing in my soul. I heard a symphony playing quietly in the background, I rested on Vicuna wool and slept like a drunken baby.

It was as if I was living my best life - right then and right there.

I was comfortable, happy, and content. It was like this magical world had taken me out of the dirt and washed me clean. Like the weight of a thousand worlds was suddenly lifted from my shoulders, and I could fly. Maybe even soar.

I walked around for a while, as the field of emerald grass filled up all around me with beautiful, exotic flowers. All at once, as if they were put there just then, at that moment. Just for me.

No one was anywhere near and there was absolute silence all around me. I was alone, but I did not feel lonely. I felt free.

Then, the silence was broken by the sound of smoke piped from an engine. My bus was waiting. Even though no one told me, I knew somewhere inside that it was time to go. I made sure to walk as slowly as I could on the way there, taking in as much of the scenery as I could.

I stepped on board, looking down at my shoes. That's when I guess reality (and the paranoia that comes from getting stoned) starts to set in.

I messed up. I made a mistake. I shouldn't have gotten back on that bus.

I yelled back up to the front, "Hey, man! Listen… I have to go back. Is there any way you can turn around and drop me back off?"

"No," the driver responded, in that same murky voice as before. "We're almost there. Too late to turn back now. Sorry."

"You can't make an exception? Just this once, please?"

"No. Like I said, I'm sorry, kid."

I pouted alone in my seat and looked out the window on the last few miles of the journey home. I saw the stars flash before me and memories of my life. The love and the loss. The mistakes and the misery.

That's what I was going back to now. I had forsaken paradise for the rubble left of my empty life on Earth. Now, I had a second chance to be a two-time loser.

I stepped off the bus with my head down, and immediately felt the cold winter air. I turned around to say something sarcastic to the driver when I heard:

"Hey, don't worry. I'll pick you up again someday. But I think you need to take care of some things here first. Then? I'll be back for you."

I smiled and turned to thank him. That's when I finally got a glimpse of his face for the first time.

It was me. *I was the bus driver.* The whole time, and I never even knew it.

---------- THE END ----------

ACKNOWLEDGEMENTS:

I don't think I could start off anywhere else but with the one person in my life who understands me the most - my loving wife, Mickey. Thank you for always being there to not only listen to my silly ideas, but also to my venting. I don't know how you're able to put up with it sometimes, but I appreciate that you do. I love you with all my heart.

My four daughters: Chelsea, Hailey, Gwyndoln, and Regan, as well as my grandchildren, Brenton and Emberly, are treasures in this world. I hope you live your lives knowing the value of self-worth. Never, ever let anyone convince you that you are less than you are. Hold your head up high, stay above the fray, and always know that you can survive anything just by believing in yourself.

My father, William S. Boman, who has been my steady rock since the day I was born. Many young men grow up idolizing sports stars or entertainers; I didn't need to. I idolized my father, because I couldn't have asked for a better man to look up to.

My grandmother, Eva Boman - the most wonderful lady I've ever known. Your spirit walks beside me every day. And in some way, you've been there for every single word I have ever typed. I love you, and thank you for all the blessings you added to my life.

Uncle John, Aunt Joni, Josh, and Jaidra - you are my family, my heart, and my support system. No one could ask for better people in their lives than you. I have been blessed to share your last name.

My best friend and business partner, Michael Melchor, has provided me with so much of his wisdom and guidance over the years.

Mike, you've been like a brother-in-arms, as well as a brother in life. The projects that we worked on over the years gave me the fuel to branch out on my own, but on a bigger scale. For that, I am truly grateful, honored, and humbled.

To Sean, thank you for always being the guy who looked out for me, even in times when I couldn't look out for myself. You taught me a lot of lessons I didn't realize until I finally, REALLY grew up. I know inside that I'm indebted to you forever.

To my lifelong friend Mikey, the laughs and jokes we shared together over the years influenced a lot of the humor in this book. So, in many ways, you are a major part of it.

Travis --- we have lived the first half of our lives in the dark, searching for something more. Now, let's live the second half healthy, wealthy, and wise.

To John Falkenhein and the staff at The County Journal, you are an invaluable part of my story. I had my re-birth as a writer in that building almost ten years ago, and I would not have embarked on this journey again if it wasn't for my time there. So, I will always be grateful for the opportunities my experience there has afforded me.

Various mentors over the years in journalism and media have given me the kind of advice that you simply can't pay for.

However, I would be remiss if I didn't prominently mention pro football editor Howard Balzer, the late baseball journalist Bob Broeg, and legendary pro wrestling editor Bill Apter.

Broadcasters Jay Randolph Jr, Brian McKenna, Joe DeNiro, Jason Fink, Dave Rapp, Allen 'Baby O' Horton, and Bob Fescoe, among so many others.

Naming all the people in St. Louis media that helped me over the years would take up a book by itself. All I can really do is just pass along my sincerest thank you to all.

And with humble appreciation, I must thank my original journalism teacher, Mr. Herman Albers. You're easily one of the most intelligent and entertaining men I've ever known, and you molded my writing style.

To my friends and family in professional wrestling and pro sports, watching your greatness and amazing ability allows me to always be the kid who 'ran away and joined the circus'. I credit my time in and around that world as teaching me more about life than life itself.

To all the friends, schoolmates, and acquaintances I've been lucky enough to meet over the years, all I can say is that I'm grateful as any man could possibly be.

Being around so many fascinating people on life's everyday journeys has provided me with a lot of lessons about life, love, laughter, and loss.

Their stories - and mine - all came together in this book.
So? *Merci* **for all the memories.**

Made in the USA
Monee, IL
16 June 2023